NAVIGATING DEFINING MOMENTS:

"As a counselor and pastoral psychologist, I am amazed at both the wisdom and practical insights Dr. Mercidieu Phillips and Kelvin McCree has for you within these pages. Read it, do it, and your life and relationships will improve, grow, and be blessed."

--Dr. Larry Keefauver,
bestselling author and International Teacher

"Dr. Mercidieu Phillips and Kelvin McCree give us a timely word about how we need to approach our world in a brave new way. The world has changed, and we need guides to help us navigate our way forward. I highly recommend this book for anyone who is alive during this Global Pandemic. That means this book is for EVERYONE!"

--Pastor Matt Keller
Next Level Church, Fort Myers, FL
Next Level Relational Network

"This book is an intellectual GPS that will reroute you to a better future. If you don't have a sense of urgency, then get ready to activate and navigate unlimited possibilities."

---Simon T. Bailey,
author of Shift Your Brilliance

"A defining moment is that point at which the essential nature or character of a person is revealed. Everybody has defining moments, but not everybody navigates them successfully. In Navigating Defining Moments, Dr. Mercidieu Phillips and Mr. Kelvin McCree insightfully and with clarity provide both the instrument and the plan to successfully navigate the defining moments of your life. Whatever your defining moment, the rich content of this book more than delivers on the promise of its title. Prepare to be empowered to seize opportunities of unforeseen change! "

Dr. William L. Glover,
author of Thirty Days of Excellence.

"Navigating Defining Moments provides the reader with practical assessments for understanding themselves and how they encounter life challenges. The Practical questions Kelvin and Phil provide offer clarity for the reader to see the benefits of growing through life's greatest challenges. If you tend to make excuses, this book will take them away!"

Bill Mutz,
Mayor of Lakeland Florida

Navigating DEFINING MOMENTS

*The opportunities of an
Unforeseen Change*

DR. MERCIDIEU PHILLIPS
AND KELVIN MCCREE

XULON PRESS

Xulon Press
2301 Lucien Way #415
Maitland, FL 32751
407.339.4217
www.xulonpress.com

© 2020 by Dr. Mercidieu Phillips and Kelvin McCree

Edited by Xulon Press
Editorial Director: Dr. Larry Keefauver
www.doctorlarry.og

Paperback ISBN-13: 978-1-6312-9851-6
Dust Jacket ISBN-13: 978-1-6322-1727-1

Ebook ISBN-13: 978-1-6312-9852-3
Audiobook ISBN-13: 978-1-6322-1728-8

DEDICATION

Dr. Phil Phillips

TO MY COACH and mentor, Dr. Steve Smith: You have greatly impacted my life and journey towards becoming a resonant leader. You have helped shaped me while helping me understand the keys to lasting leadership. I am forever grateful to you and Shirley.

TO EMMA PHILLIPS: Your courage and determination as a cancer survivor laced my life with so many intangible elements of faith, courage and grace. Thank you for silently teaching me what it means to courageously navigate defining moments. Your example is transformational and inspiring.

TO BERTA PLANCHER: Your presence in my life though limited by life's unpredictability, left a stain on my soul and eternal lessons to be learned by generations. Thank you for being gracious in the face of daunting adversity. My heartfelt thanks to you!

TABLE OF CONTENTS

ACKNOWLEDGMENTS

Dr. Phil Phillips

THE DUTY OF writing a book of this kind is never the work of one individual. My circle of supporters enlarges each time I glance outside of the peephole of gratitude. I have to thank Emma, for her unfailing sense of support and encouragement and allowing me to always pursue the vision and ideas I constantly share and then chase after. She gives up countless hours of being with me so I can focus and properly capture with clarity the thoughts I wish the readers to engage with. My son Jehiel and daughter Hadassah who inspire me to never become complacent because their destiny is closely tied to what I offer them and the watching world.

Thanks to my amazing team of servant leaders at ACF including Jean Denavard Tranquilus and Bjorn B Burrows who carry so much of the load so I can adequately shoulder the task of leadership to so many others. You all are an amazing group to whom I owe an eternal appreciation. To my brilliant research assistants, Tatiana Fortune and Nerlynn Etienne. You two know my expectations better than anyone and you always rise to meet them with your meticulous manner of ensuring that all is done correctly. A Big thank you to my executive administrative assistant, Wilma Davilus for always keeping my rhythm of purpose moving in a progressive direction. I owe an insurmountable debt of gratitude to Mack Jno-Charles, Carla Narcisse, Dr. Patricia Schwarz and so many other close advisors, cheerleaders and partakers. The list is too long so please find yourself in this loaded basket of gratitude.

Thanks also to my countless supporters and friends in #DPMNATION who answer the call each time to push this vision forward. I appreciate each one of you.

Thanks for my late father, Wesley Phillips who indirectly taught me the value of hard work and what it means to live a life fueled by courage, determination and grit. The latter years of our life together taught me the secret elements of success.

Finally, thank you to my partner in this work, Kelvin McCree who agreed to take this journey with me in order to help others define and design their own moment of productivity. I have learned to appreciate and admire the knowledge and sense of calling that you possess. Thanks for being authentic and an inspiration to me.

Kelvin McCree

THE WORLD IS an amazing place thanks to people who recognize their calling to invest in others, to lead them and inspire them. Thank you to the mentors and coaches who continue to innovate, cultivate and help others realize their dreams. To my friend and mentor, Simon T. Bailey, the pivot I made during the Covid-19 pandemic was a direct result of your challenge to me, and it was that moment where I found even greater appreciation for change.

To all the individuals, organizations, corporations and governmental agencies I have had the opportunity to serve, I want to thank you for allowing me to serve you, learn from you and gain greater understanding of what you face during change. Without the experiences and support from you, the knowledge shared in this book would not exist.

To Dr. Phil, you are a leader of leaders! Being asked to Co-Author this book is such a privilege and I am grateful for the opportunity to come alongside you and share in this incredible work. Working with you on this project has been incredibly fun!

To my children, of all the accolades and achievements in my life, the one thing that matters most is raising great human beings. I love you both and hearing you call me dad makes my heart sing.

Finally, to my amazing wife Evette. You have epito-mized partnership. From listening to my ideas, being my sounding board and tolerating my constant desire to create, you have always locked arms with me and said, yes. You are one of the smartest, most talented people on the planet, yet you harness your brilliance with humility. Thank you for your eternal love!

FOREWORD FOR
NAVIGATING DEFINING MOMENTS

"IT WAS MARCH 12, 2020, I was a flight returning home after speaking at a leadership conference. By then, we were wiping down our seats on airplanes etc. However, no one was wearing masks or socially distancing. Little did I know that that would be my last flight for months. I'm used to averaging 170-190 flights a year! Not this year.

What happened? Disruption!

For a few years I've tried to slow down my leadership consulting business. I've had a few very well organized strategic plans, but they all failed—till now. When everything shifted to online delivery, it evened the playing field with all my clients. Regardless of what they paid me, now it was all online. During these difficult COVID-days, I have spoken at leadership conferences, consulted with all my clients (in fact, my business grew), preached at churches, taught webinars and did interviews literally all over the world. In addition to that, I launched a leadership journal, AVAIL, and expanded my online leadership institute.

Why? Because of what my friends Dr. Mercidieu Phillips and Kelvin McCree teach in this book. NAVIGATING DEFINING MOMENTS: *The Opportunities of an Unforeseen Change* is more than a book leveraging this moment in time. The message is simple yet not simplistic. The question for every reader is probing and even uncomfortable: *"Is this period of time going to find you a good steward of opportunities or someone who wasted opportunities?"*

These are defining moments indeed. Navigating them is not easy. This principle laden book will light your pathway so you can lean into "opportunities of unforeseen change."

Dr. Sam Chand
Leadership Consultant and
Author of Harnessing The Power of Tension
www.samchand.com

[Introduction]

CHANGE VS. DISRUPTION

What is change?

> ***Change*** *is described as: "To make the form, nature, content, future of something, different from what is or from what it would be if left alone."*

WE ARE LIVING in an era where constant change is the new norm. Social media posts have a shelf life of no more than two hours at the most. Carefully produced songs remain on a billboard or popular music chart for an average of three months.

We function in a world where change is common, expected, and applauded. However, despite the constant nature of change, change is not always a naturally accepted reality. It is processed through the filter of one's present circumstance or position in life.

Try This…

Stand with your feet a little apart.
Cross your arms in front of your chest.
Note which arm is crossed over the top of the other arm.
Now, re-cross your arms and change it so the other arm
is now on the top.

*Was it comfortable or uncomfortable to change the way you
cross your arms?*

**There are times we seek much-needed change and
then there are times when change simply comes to us.**

Forced Change

Far away in a relatively unknown Chinese city to
Westerners, a global force of change penetrated the
195 countries of the world. It shattered the confidence
of once robust world superpowers. It put the insuffi-
ciency of all medical and scientific advances on notice.
This simple, yet powerful reality reduced leaders of great
nations to mere spectators and questioners of something
that political savvy could not wrestle to the ground.

This devastating phenomenon placed a dynamite like
explosive power at the base of once failure-proof econ-
omies. It shamefully tested the capacity of modern soci-
eties' responsive power. It left doors of churches of all
sizes, faiths, and denominations closed. It forced the
closure of mosques, synagogues, and temples. It suspended the patronizing of bustling shopping malls,
emptied once crowded streets, gutted busy restaurants,
and left businesses of each imaginable size scrambling

for new client reaching strategies. It quickly introduced consumers to curbside only service, touchless shopping experiences, and delivery only options.

The traffic at the world's busiest airports came to a screeching halt. Hotels heard the blaring silence of empty lobbies, rooms, and suites. Family parks such as Disney World and Busch Gardens halted all the fun in the face of seriousness. Transportation companies parked vehicles, grounded aircraft, docked maritime vessels, and accepted the reduced flow of income. This little but powerful enemy left sporting arenas hollow and shut down the lights on stages where performers had found pulsating energy through the entertainment of the masses. It canceled entire school years and eliminated high school and university graduations everywhere.

This reality, called Coronavirus simply came to bear the name, COVID19. The historic proportion of this pandemic will lace the annals of history with irreplaceable markings. It has permanently left an indelible mark on the fabric of our souls in more ways than one. Its indiscriminate reach has touched lives from the neonatal wing of hospitals to the quiet rooms of nursing and private homes.

This global pandemic affected over three million people and ended the earthly experience of 375,000 people in just six short but painful months! This disruption forced everyone to adopt new personal hygiene habits, introduced us to the new term "social distancing," and elevated the importance of frontline heroes, essential workers, and especially those in the medical field.

This pandemic brought with it the powerful reality of forced change!

Describe Your Feelings When You Were Forced to...

Change the way you shopped

_____

_____

Change your daily exercise routine

_____

_____

Change your eating habits

_____

_____

Change personal hygiene procedures

_____

_____

Change your work environment

_____

_____

What is Disruption?

In the interest of this discourse, we want to introduce you to the term "**disruption**" in lieu of "change." Disruption is defined as: "forcible separation or division into parts." We use this term because what happened with this pandemic is not simply a change, but a major disruption. It was a disruption to everything we have ever labeled as normal. It is a "forced separation" from all that we once cherished as routine. It is a violent ripping away of closely held assumptions and dearly cherished entitlements.

In the face of such a seismic disruption, the temptation to fall into the trap of resignation or situational accommodation is ever-present. The convenient and generous offerings of complacency are always available.

In every real and life challenging crisis, the people on the receiving end always have the privilege of two alternatives.

Which Alternative Did You Choose…
(Circle your answer.)

Rise or fold?
Grow or shrink?
Pivot or remain idle?
Accept things as is or create your own disruption in the midst of an unforeseen crisis?

This book is about providing you with a life-altering friendly guide as you navigate this new normal. It is our selfless and generous offering of practical principles designed to assist you on this journey of self-discovery, purpose, passion, and destiny. This book is meant to serve as a mental electrical shock to jolt you to another realm of limitless possibilities. The numerous pages you will peruse are intended to illuminate your mind, jump-start your will, and activate your innate abilities to seize this disruption as the opportunity you have always been waiting for.

We move forward with the hope that these chapters will consistently create discomfort, while challenging you to a better and more prosperous life experience. We carefully desire that these words will land on you as a breath of fresh air. We pen these words as an invitation for you to escape the ferocious grip of fear of the unknown and to lend yourself to the broad horizon of "better" that is yearning to meet you. We unashamedly and selfishly wish you will embrace the challenge to grow past your current level of acceptance, by creating new space for the abundant provisions of what awaits you beyond the borders of the status quo.

As you begin this journey with us, we acknowledge the inner forces of resistance through the loud and at times boisterous voice of complacency. However, we thank you in advance for accepting the invitation to navigate change, while making new waves in the bottomless ocean of life-giving possibilities. In so doing, you are deciding that you are ready for more and demonstrating that your desire for the unknown has been awakened.

Say Out Loud…

❖ I will seize this disruption as the opportunity I have always been waiting for.

❖ I will embrace the challenge to grow past my current level of acceptance.

Let's NAVIGATE!

[Chapter 1]

SHIFT HAPPENS

Mercidieu Phillips

*"Stubborn problems always require a
shift in paradigm."*
- Jamelle Sanders

IT WAS A beautiful and pleasant Tuesday morning
as school-age children settled into their respective classrooms for a day of gaining new information. Most businesses had already flipped the sign on the front door
from closed to open. The Stock market was bustling,
and the spirit of America was as strong as ever. In fact,
the President of the United States of America found
himself in the midst of a joyous classroom in Tampa,
Florida with stargazing children. It was just like any
other ordinary day in the world, especially in the USA.
It was an ordinary day when husbands kissed their wives
and children goodbye, as they hurried off to work. It was
like any other day when school buses made their rounds
and picked up and dropped off students running to the
playground or their classrooms. That morning, every
airport around the country probably went through their

normal opening procedures. Those responsible for the safe transport of people on their aircraft without a doubt conducted their mandatory safety checks. All in all, it was just another day in the USA and around the world.

Then it happened! Across television screens, regular morning shows were being interrupted with the horrifying news and images of commercial aircraft crashing into buildings designed for people, not airplanes. News of the World Trade Center towers crumbling like playhouses constructed from the inferior materials kids revel in felt, sounded, and looked surreal. Further, the idea that there were two more sites of horror, namely the US Pentagon in Washington, D.C. and in Shanksfield, PA, was simply too much to handle.

The United States of America and the world had just witnessed the visible manifestation of evil at its climax. The world had just been welcomed to the now famous three-digit identity of fear, massive loss, hatred, vulnerability, and evil known simply as 9/11. September 11, 2001, is a day that will never be forgotten because it is one of those "where were you moments."

The world shifted that day and America was upended and catapulted into a new reality that would mandate wholesale changes that still remain a part of our everyday lives years later. From the tedious pat-downs at the airport during routine travel, to the unlimited access and surveillance power afforded to world governments, on 9/11 a shift happened

The Shift

When I speak of shift, I am referring to more than what is described as a sudden movement. I am speaking of an unforeseen, unwanted, and uncomfortable occurrence that necessitates an adjustment to life as normal. One of the most certain things in life is the idea that nothing is permanent. Sudden shifts can be the result of uncontrollable natural disasters such as hurricanes, tornadoes, flooding, tsunamis, and earthquakes. For some, a shift may come in the form of a medical diagnosis or the unexpected loss of a loved one. It may come through the news of a change in your employment status, a relocation of the entire family, or via the painful announcement of a divorce. Regardless of how a shift happens, it is usually a disturbance of one's sense of peace. It is a forceful disturbance of an accepted rhythm. Shifts shock the normalcy of life. They place pressure on previously held priorities as well as preferences. Shifts enter our guarded space like a federal interrogator seeking closely held secrets. They silently interview us about our worldview. They force us to really think about the value scale of our lives. A shift is a mirror that provides a reflection of self and what really matters.

*"The shift is a collective transformation
consisting of the sum of each individual's step into the
new reality.
Each person, in their own time, is moving into a stage of
consciousness
which brings a wider vista and awareness which springs
from the heart."*
– Owen Waters

What Is Attitude?

Attitude is a small thing that makes a big difference.

Attitude is defined as one's perception and interpretation of reality and world events. Attitude has three components—thoughts, feelings, and behaviors. World renown evangelical leader, Dr. Charles Swindoll noted this truth when he said, "Life is 10% what happens to me and 90% how I respond to it."

The irrefutable truth about life is that there is no such thing as an "attitude-less" person on earth. When a shift happens in your life, it is an invitation to discover just what type of attitude you possess. It will reveal if you are the carrier of a positive or a negative attitude.

During my years of leadership development and executive coaching, I have heard countless references to people who are labeled as having a negative or a positive attitude. People who exude a negative attitude will most likely view a shift as a setback, an unwelcome occurrence, or a fatal blow. They process the shift through the polluted filter of past failures and unfinished projects. They quickly descend to the mental basement that houses feelings of failure, self-defeat, and disappointment. They may even befriend the debilitating notion of resignation.

On the other hand, the person who experiences the same shift, but possesses a positive attitude will quickly put on the glasses of limitless opportunities and open doors. A positive attitude is understood as being optimistic in life-bending situations. It generally refers to how someone chooses to view an active occurrence. It defines how they interact with self and others. They process information constructively. The carrier of a positive attitude exudes a life-giving and infectious hopefulness based on how they can see the boundless good, even in trying and difficult situations. They are the ones who raise and fly the flag of forward-thinking by using the winds of adversity as fuel.

Be Honest with Yourself…

Ask yourself about the recent shifts in your life due to the Corona Virus:

➢ *Did I view it with a debilitating setback attitude?*

➢ *Did I view it with a constructive attitude?*

➢ *Was I able to move from a negative to a positive attitude?*

What Are the Health Benefits of a Positive Attitude?

Research has shown that a positive attitude can provide monumental benefits to one's physical body. It has been shown that a positive attitude greatly reduces the stress load and creates greater stamina. Science even speaks of how a positive attitude contributes to the overall strength of the immune system.

> "A positive attitude can improve your immune system and may help you live longer, according to a University of Queensland study. The research, published in Psychology and Aging

has found that older people who focused on positive information were more likely to have stronger immune systems. Lead researcher Dr. Elise Kalokerinos, from UQ's School of Psychology, said a positive attitude played an important role in healthy aging."

"POSITIVE THINKING CAN IMPROVE THE IMMUNE SYSTEM.

With recent events worldwide, current medical research has focused on ways the immune system functions and can be improved. In a similar effect, psychological studies show that people recover from illnesses such as flu and colds faster and are less symptomatic than compared with people who have a more negative thought process."

THINK OUTSIDE THE BOX...

➤ *Diagnose your work attitude.*

➤ *Prescribe an antidote for any negative attitudes.*

➤ *Design a "diet" of positive energy that will feed, fuel, and energize your soul.*

The positive person is someone who chooses to use the difficult moment as a time to create new plans, dream more audacious dreams, and establish goals.

Imagine working for an organization where the senior leadership, middle management, and employees embrace a culture of positive attitude. Picture yourself spending eight to ten hours a day breathing in air filled with positive thinkers, dreamers, implementers, and doers. Like nicotine to an addict, this positive energy will feed and energize your soul. It is imperative for the executive, manager, supervisor, or team leader who wants to see a more profitable organization, to adopt and promote a positive attitude.

The disruption of COVID19 provided an X-ray machine to closely examine and reveal attitudes. The revelation of your attitude is either the affirming element you already possess or the rude awakening to the much-needed change that is due. While you may not have control over the events of life, you do have sole control over how you view and navigate these events. The ink on these pages is seeking to make its way to your mind as you choose your personal disposition.

Are You Aware of Yourself?

> *"What is necessary to change a person
> is to change his awareness of himself."*
> - Abraham Maslow[1]

Any change or shift of major significance begins with a heightened sense of awareness. I would dare to say that awareness is the mother of newness. The ability to develop a high degree of consciousness leads people to escape the stingy traps of ignorance and complacency. Awareness forcefully taps the dormant cells of creativity while increasing the flow of innovative juices. It is the trusted guide that takes the willing individual from point A to point B.

Fill in this Diagram to get From Point A to Point B...

Point A: First Action to reach next step is:	Next Action needed to reach next step is:	Next Action to reach Point B is:
_____	_____	_____

Awareness demands a forward-moving action, and an insatiable desire for greater.

Psychologists and mental health experts across the spectrum mostly agree on the explanation of awareness as: "the state of being conscious of something. More specifically, is the ability to directly know and perceive, to feel or to be cognizant of events."[2] Sigmund Freud greatly contributed to the development of this idea when he made the attempt to explain consciousness as a three-level reality. His three levels are: consciousness, preconscious, and unconscious. Without boring you with a prolonged exercise on psychology and risk having you put this much-needed book away, I will engage your mind rather on why it is critically important for you to develop and traffic in a stream of progressive and constructive consciousness. The audacity to become a steady and faithful patron of awareness will yield an ROI (Return On Investment) that will conveniently place you in the arms of success now and in the future.

In their book, "Reframing Organizations," authors Lee Bolman and Terrance Deal introduce an interesting term called the "curse of cluelessness." They make the following observation:

> *Year after year, the best and brightest managers maneuver or meander their way to the apex of enterprises great and small. Then they do really dumb things. How do bright people turn out so dim? One theory is that they're too smart for their own good. Fiendberg and Tarrant (1995) label it the "self-destructive intelligence syndrome." They argue that smart people act stupid because of personality flaws like, pride, arrogance, and unconscious desires to fail. Intellectually challenged people have as many psychological problems as the best and brightest. The primary source of cluelessness is not personality or IQ. We're at sea whenever our sense-making efforts fail us. If our image of a situation is wrong, our actions will be wide of the mark as well. But if we don't realize our image is incorrect, we don't understand why we don't get what we hoped for."[3]*

The development of personal awareness is a tremendous benefit to the one who takes on the critical task of creating such space for the purpose of experiencing positive change.

Wayne Dyer gives an interesting thought to ponder when he states, "If we want to move from disenchantment to inspiration, or from apathy and indifference to passion and enthusiasm, then it's necessary to alter our awareness of ourselves."[4]

Picture This…

> ➢ *Sketch out what your new normal looks like.*
>
> ➢ *Think of ways you can create space in your life to experience the positive change needed to achieve it.*

The *new normal* will demand a new way of seeing and perceiving. Change is the only constant and must be the accepted conductor of our complete being.

Are You Disciplined in Measured Urgency?

There has been a popular saying that, "the early bird gets the worm." The challenges we now face carry a potent mixture of both fear and excitement. They are hazardous and at the same time adventurous. The reduction of the global community creates the unprecedented openings of greater opportunities for all who wish to tap into the abundant pool of growth, development, and significance.

In his classic book "Leading Change," John Kotter identifies the necessity of creating a sense of urgency for a company or organization when he writes, "Establishing a sense of urgency is crucial to gaining needed cooperation. With complacency high, transformations usually go nowhere because few people are even interested in working on the change problem."[5]

Let me be clear that urgency is not the same as reckless impatience to pre-mature behavior. The sense of urgency I am submitting to you is one that is based on a calculated and well-researched plan of action. It is a decisive resolve that is birthed from the deep crevices of one's heart and desire for enhanced success and reality.

My Action Plan…

- ✓ Research
- ✓ Calculations
- ✓ Tools Needed
- ✓ Assistance Needed
- ✓ Finances Needed
- ✓ Timeframe

A crisis of the proportion of COVID19 places a demand on one's mind and sense of purpose. It comes as the neurological stimulant that jumpstarts the never before low-lying nerves of steel, courage, and fearlessness. Urgency is the fuel that ignites passion, vision, drive, and failure-bending power. The person who operates with a sense of urgency creates an unbeatable edge over the competition.

**Urgency is the antithesis
of complacency.**

Dr. Martin Luther King Jr. is best known as a fierce civil rights leader. However, he was more known as the "Moses" of the African-American community in the United States for the manner in which he led the exodus out of the dark period of slavery. He conducted his mission with a clear sense of urgency. The marches he led, the sit-ins, the eloquent speeches, and the let-ters from the Birmingham jail were all by-products of something the average person could not see, urgency. It is this sense of a "now moment" that provided the impetus to stare threats, name-calling, vitriolic rhet-oric, and even death in the face and not waver. The abundant provisions of that sense of urgency is for-ever etched in the fabric of America and afforded the watching world a much-needed template on how even the most daunting endeavors can yield transforma-tional experience.

Nevertheless, it is never just enough to have a sense of urgency. It is crucial to embrace urgency as a way of living. The fast-moving world we now find our-selves in provides no one with the luxury of being "normal" in thinking or being. The constant movement of information through ever-changing technology cre-ates a nauseating effect to both understand and keep up. The present reality of a world deeply immersed in the world of the unknown will produce a generation of game-changers who understand that this is their moment to rise and to expand their reach.

Are you a gamechanger?

Is Acceptance One of Your Attributes?

When helping people process the various stages of loss or grief, one of the critical elements of this journey is the idea of acceptance. With any major shift in some-one's life, whether positive or negative, acceptance of the change is necessary for the full experience of the said change. The disruption created by the pandemic of COVID19 is still a difficult notion to embrace. The massive loss of life, the change in jobs due to companies downsizing, and the change in how businesses adapt to a new customer service experience are all huge alterations for us to process and eventually accept.

We are all humans who must deal with an emotional side to our existence regardless of the incredible advances which science has made. When things occur, unfortunately, they don't stay suspended in time. They land on real people. While some may choose to employ an avoidance mechanism as a way to cope, conscious people cannot eternally ignore reality. Major shifts or changes land differently on each person.

At the onset of the global crisis created by COVID19, not everyone took it at face value. Some thought it was a hoax while others believed it was the end of the world. Store shelves were raided for such mundane things like toilet paper and hand sanitizer. The disinfectant sections of stores resembled a fresh war zone. Banks were depleted of hard cash, gas stations were overrun with lines of cars waiting to stock up on fuel, and department stores glared at empty aisles once filled with shoppers looking for that great deal. These were all outward symptoms of what was really happening inside of people's minds. The behaviors of frantic consumers were subtle hints of how everyone was processing the "hit" they were taking.

Processing the "Hit"…

Circle the phrases that best describe how you processed COVID19:

Hoax   Panic   Frantic   Hoard   Isolation   Fear

Disbelief   Anger   Avoidance   Acceptance   Adapted

Are You Optimistic or Pessimistic?

Acceptance is the launching pad for meaningful decisions and progress. It is the catalytic force that creates an eruption of new directional thinking. It creates a burst of energy that catapults one way or another. For the progressive thinker and opportunist, it creates windows, doors, cracks, and openings for a new idea. They move with lightning speed to tap into what they have made an agreement with.

On the other hand, for the pessimistic and gun-shy person, the acceptance has the total opposite effect. It provides an opening to sink into a despondent state, embrace defeat, and make a covenant with a mindset of failure and doom. From the sharp cutting lines of this work, I hope you are seeing and feeling that I deeply desire that you choose the option of being a progressive and opportunistic individual, rather than make the convenient choice of the latter.

Life-altering moments are buffet lines for those whose insatiable appetite yearn for growth and success. You have the rare opportunity to become a part of that line with just the resolve of accepting that a new era is upon us now!

●— *Pause and Reflect…*

Review the Key Points highlighted in this chapter. Journal what revelation you received from each one and how it will affect how you look at and deal with change and disruptions in your life.

> ➤ **There are times we seek much-needed change and then there are times when change simply comes to us.**

> ➤ **This pandemic brought with it the powerful reality of forced change!**

> ➤ **Attitude is a small thing that makes a big difference.**

> ➤ **Positive Thinking Can Improve the Immune System**

> ➤ **Awareness demands a forward-moving action and an insatiable desire for greater.**

> ➤ **Urgency is the antithesis of complacency.**

Say Out Loud…

(Learning happens with **Frequency**, **Intensity** and **Repetition**. So, this week, repeat these declarations loudly to yourself in front of a mirror at least 6 times daily.)

> ❖ *I am a game-changer!*

> ❖ *I will rise, not fold!*

> ❖ *I will grow, not shrink!*

❖ *I will pivot, not remain idle!*

❖ *I will fly the flag of forward-thinking by using the winds of adversity as fuel.*

❖ *I choose to use difficult moments to create new plans, dream more audacious dreams, and establish goals.*

❖ *I will embrace urgency as a way of living.*

❖ *I choose the option of being a progressive and opportunistic individual.*

[Chapter 2]

PRISONERS OF THE MOMENT

Mercidieu Phillips

*"I am not a product of my circumstances.
I am a product of my decisions."*
—Stephen Covey

EVERY PRISONER HAS one goal in mind constantly! How do I break free from this situation at hand? Prison is not a place that anyone with an ounce of common sense would voluntarily decide to go, even though there are many people who frequently return for several sentences.

In the twinkling of an eye, anyone can become the prisoner of a moment, good or bad. Like real prisons, moments of great crisis create opportunities to become captive in a way that is usually not healthy. Threatening moments causes great fear, anxiety, concern, and worry, which often lead individuals to unwanted or never imagined places. They not only lead them there, but once there, they tend to overstay. There are far too many people who allow moments to paralyze them and take them hostage. A moment of great crisis can create mind blocking clouds that prohibit the possibility of thinking that a storm doesn't last forever.

The ability to place moments in perspective is critical to the full enjoyment of life and its challenges. The propensity to become irrationally overwhelmed by the current reality does create harm to the promises of tomorrow. The unpleasant and negative moments of life are always temporary, but we can make the fatal mistake of making them last longer based on where we place in them in our lives. John Maxwell noted a simple truth when said, "Success and failure have one thing in common, they both don't last forever."

The person who enters that "cell" take with them a mental picture of what is going on inside of them and all around them. This resolution of this picture is usually distorted thus creating a view that is personally unacceptable to their eyes. Further, they take maps of blocked passages, barricaded opportunities, and walled off streets. They often don't see the promises of tomorrow and settle for the comfort of a prison cell that quickly becomes a trusted place of safety.

Even the brightest and sharpest make the deadly mistake of putting on the jumpsuit of despair and hopelessness while taking their mugshot with failure.

Does this describe your condition today?
Is this where you want to be tomorrow?

The Four Prison Cells:

Fear

We are all familiar with the famous saying by President Franklin D. Roosevelt during his inaugural address in 1933, "There is nothing to fear but fear itself." Fear is a God-given emotion that alerts us that there is an imminent danger or threat to our welfare or well-being. The feeling of fear provides us with much needed data about real issues one should pay close attention to. It is not a sign of weakness or cowardness to experience and express fear. Our emotions are gifts given by God to help us live healthy and whole lives. While fear is often associated with negative vibes, it can actually be utilized for the growth and betterment of one's overall experiential journey.

The real issue begins when fear becomes both the master and conductor of your movements, decisions, and posture. It turns into a serious problem when fear isn't counterbalanced with other present realities. For example, someone can become such a prisoner of the fear of losing their employment or income that they fall into a deep depression that begins to affect the people around them. This person may choose to miss out on significant family gatherings and events as they voluntarily choose to isolate themselves and continually breathe in the toxic air created by their own thinking.

In choosing this stance, this person could fail to see all the good things that are happening around them. They can't take the time to appreciate the extra time at home with the kids, their mate, and the rare opportunity to slow down. They make the fatal mistake of allowing fear to acquire the patent to their emotional brand. Further, they hand the keys to their heart to fear and afford it unlimited access to their heart.

Evaluate Your Outlook on Fear:

Do I see fear as a sign of weakness?
Does fear keep me from appreciating events around me?
Does fear dictate my daily routine?

When properly understood, fear is a necessary "check engine" light on the dashboard of life, but it must never be allowed to dictate the direction you take as result of its far-reaching tentacles. The process of breaking out of this prison cell first begins with the realization that you are there in the first place.

In my many speaking opportunities, I have often proposed the idea that the most important ability to own is the awareness of self, place, and pace. The person who can develop the capacity to always locate self will win the game of confusion.

Self: Am I in the prison of fear?
Place: What has caused me to remain paralyzed in this prison?
Pace: How do I shatter the chains that have held me in fear?

After you realize that you may be meandering in this cell, the next step is to decide to move beyond the once paralyzing elements associated with fear. Making decisions is a daily personal responsibility that everyone has. The power that resides in this ability is strong enough to shatter the chains of slavery to such a cruel ruler such as fear. In addition, deciding to do something about fear, places a sharp pair of scissors in your hand to split the strong ropes of helplessness!

> **Decisions made for the forward progress of self often serve as the bulldozer that clears the path to productivity and stability. Use this to release yourself from the fear cell!**

Declare Out Loud:

- ❖ I will move beyond the once paralyzing elements in my life associated with fear.

- ❖ I will no longer make decisions based on irrational fear.

Worry

In recent studies, it was discovered that most people suffer from high levels of anxiety. In fact, it is one of the leading causes of strokes, hypertension and heart diseases.[6] A new long-term study suggests just that the greater the anxiety, the greater the risk for stroke. Study participants who suffered the most anxiety had a 33 percent higher risk for stroke compared to those with the lowest anxiety levels, the researchers found.[7] If stress itself is a risk factor for heart disease, it could be because chronic stress exposes your body to unhealthy, persistently elevated levels of stress hormones like adrenaline and cortisol. Studies also link stress to changes in the way blood clots, which increases the risk of heart attack.[8]

Having too much stress, for too long, is bad for your heart. If you're often stressed, and you don't have good ways to manage it, you are more likely to have heart disease, high blood pressure, chest pain, or irregular heartbeats. The stress itself can be a problem. It raises your blood pressure, and it's not good for your body to constantly be exposed to stress hormones. Studies also link stress to changes in the way blood clots, which makes a heart attack more likely. The way you handle stress also matters. If you respond to it in unhealthy ways such as smoking, overeating, or not exercising that makes matters worse. On the other hand, if you exercise, connect with people, and find meaning despite the stress, that makes a difference in your emotions and in your body.[9]

Most people often get concern and worry tangled up. Concern is a legitimate level of personal responsibility. It is both a natural and common human experience. It would be fatally hazardous to remain in the company of someone who never shows any concern over anything.

However, when concern is given a promotion beyond its boundaries, this is where worry takes over. The prison cell of worry is synonymous with solitary confinement. Gaining entrance into this cell is as easy as losing your car keys. All it takes is a temporary misplacement of your feelings. Blindly following your free-flowing feelings and allowing the pressure attached to certain moments can and will lead you right in this cell.

In speaking with a client of our coaching and consulting firm, I was introduced to just how powerful and possessive worry can become. The person told me how at the onset of Covid19 which necessitated the shutting down of all businesses, their worry meter skyrocketed to unprecedented levels. This feeling of hopelessness led to a loss of appetite, stomach ulcers, and violent emotional outbursts at any and everyone who said anything that reminded them of their current reality. Sleepless nights followed as well as a rapid decline in weight. It was getting totally out of control and they needed to stop the madness.

On a video coaching session, we meticulously unpacked some of the elements contributing to this unique experience. What we discovered was that this person had managed to remove the trust they built in their capacity to establish and run a successful business. They weight of the moment crushed their inner resolve and the fast-moving clouds of uncertainty made their vision partially obscured.

Has Your Worry Meter Skyrocketed?

Answer with a simple Yes or No:

Loss of appetite

_____

Stomach ulcers

_____

Violent emotional outbursts

Sleepless nights

Rapid decline in weight

Worry has a crippling grip on those who grants it access. It can stifle faith, creativity, and any superficial level of determination. Worry is the force that seeks to paralyze thinking, stop mobility, and completely undo years of steady progress. It is the holding place for all who willingly place themselves in its debilitating care. When left unchecked, it can cancel hope and eradicate confidence.

The best way to overcome worry is to find an acceptable balance between concern and worry. You must develop the ability to manage the velocity and frequency of untrue thoughts that comes as headwind pushing you into the jagged edges of despair. You cannot and should not blindly follow your feelings that are being manipulated by the constant winds of change. The one who does not acquire this capacity usually end of hanging themselves in the cell by the cords of a broken spirit and a battered soul.

Those who find the courage to both recognize and mitigate worry, usually experience the freedom of moving about and soaring to

new heights. It is at the front of this heavy door that you must decide to stare your future in the face and turn the knob to find the greatness that this moment contains!

Limitations

When I get ready to board a jetliner for a speaking engagement or training sessions, I have a deep appreciation for all the limitations they put in place. From the highly scrutinized TSA screenings, to the weight and size of all checked carry-on bags, these efforts ensure the safety of everyone and are deeply appreciated. However, there are certain aspects of life where limitations can be very dangerous. Limitations placed on the mind as result of a challenging crisis can cause great harm to the much-needed forward progress of personal and professional advancement.

Simply stated, difficult moments come to relocate you into a setting that is beset with the generous offerings of regressive thinking, stale ideas, blocked creativity, and stagnation.

The turbulent winds of a crisis can do two things:

First, it can blow you directly into a state of being completely despondent, overwhelmed by the gravity of its presence and committed to the popular option of nothingness.

Secondly, limitations will persistently leave you in the basement of possibilities while riding high in your mental space.

Does this describe your current perception of the limitations you are experiencing due to a crisis in your life?

On the other hand, this same wind can be the only source of power someone might need to shake free from the molasses type struggle and jump right into the ocean of better. Albert Einstein said, "Adversity introduces a man to himself."[10]

The prison cell of limitations houses more than just a person, but it holds hostage the purpose and destiny that is within that person. It captures the mind of its resident and dictates how far they can go. At first, living in this cell doesn't seem to disturb much. It almost feels harmless and pain free. However, a prolonged stay begins the methodical erosion of the will and desire.

Because of its shameless obsession with delayed living, it will never willingly release you until you announce your desire to check out of its confines.

Announce Out Loud:

- ❖ I desire to check out of the confines of my self-imposed prison of limitations.

As noted in the previous chapter, a sense of urgency must provide your personal corrections officer to show you the way out of that chamber. Desire is the birthplace of change. It cannot be taught or caught, but

must come from deep within the person whose time
has come to walk out as a former inmate but now freed
to the exciting possibilities of the world.

Familiarity

The greatest threat to change is change! Most people
are reluctant to any idea of change that requires massive adjustments. On a return trip from a conference in
California, while sitting in the executive lounge at the
Dallas Fort Worth airport waiting to catch my con-
necting flight, I engaged in a conversation with a man
who was traveling for business. After we exchanged
pleasantries, he asked me about my line of work.

I told him that I am in the business of helping people
enhance their reality while reaching for their future.
He perked up in his seat as someone who was eager
to hear more. As we munched on the veggie platter
and some excellent salami with cheese and crackers, he
told me how much he hates anything that isn't familiar.
His tone confirmed for me what his mouth was saying.
He shared with me how he has only worked for two
major companies during his thirty-seven years as a sales
executive. When I told him that part of my job was to
facilitate change for others, he said you must have a lot
clients who aren't like me! Unfortunately, this man isn't
alone. There are scores of people out there who love the
convenience of familiarity.

Covid19 shook up everything that was routine and
familiar. It disturbed neatly planned plans. It upended
all that was ever considered normal. It served as a vivid

reminder that change is the one constant in life. More than that, it created what I call a "soul and mind-quake" in the same way the shifting of tectonic plates under the earth can cause catastrophic damage. Settling for the temptation of remaining in the safety bonds of what is known is a detrimental exercise on the playing field of significance.

The air of this prison cell is thick with fear of the unknown and the surrounding environment is readily poisoned with failure. Think of it this way, it takes very little effort to move in the direction of idleness. It demands very little from the person who is not too concerned with upgrading their present place in the que of life.

A disruption of this magnitude can foster the existence of a life defying dualism. There is on the one hand the opportunity to remain frozen in the quicksand of unwanted circumstances.

❖ *How did Covid19 shake up everything that was routine and familiar in your life?*

❖ *Did you find yourself in a prison cell thick with fear of the unknown?*

❖ *Did you remain frozen in quicksand of unwanted circumstances?*

Then there is the option of rise up and stare down familiarity while proudly sporting the super forward-looking lens of boldness and audacity. Refusing to live in the controlled space of familiarity is the most critical step towards completely escaping the menacing grip of nothingness. The duration is completely within the power of your personal will.

The most critical thought you will have to manage is deciding if you want to be remembered as a person who allowed a moment of crisis to become a prisoner of the yesterday or the carrier of a pioneering spirit who defies all odds. Choose wisely, your future depends on it!

◆— *Pause and Reflect…*

Life offers varying degrees of joy and pain and it is up to you how you process them. Henry Nouwen put this truth this way, "The greatest joy as well as greatest pain in living come from not only from what we live, but even more from how we think and feel what we are living."[11]

Review the Key Points highlighted in this chapter. Journal what revelation you received from each one and how it will affect how you look at and deal with change and disruptions in your life.

> ➤ **Decisions made for the forward progress of self often serve as the bulldozer that clears the path to productivity and stability. Use this to release yourself from the fear cell!**

> ➤ **Those who find the courage to both recognize and mitigate worry, usually experience the freedom of moving about and soaring to new heights. It is at the front of this heavy door**

that you must decide to stare your future in the face and turn the knob to find the greatness that this moment contains!

➢ Simply stated, difficult moments come to relocate you into a setting that is beset with the generous offerings of regressive thinking, stale ideas, blocked creativity, and stagnation.

➢ The most critical thought you will have to manage is deciding if you want to be remembered as a person who allowed a moment of crisis to become a prisoner of the yesterday or the carrier of a pioneering spirit who defies all odds. Choose wisely, your future depends on it!

Say Out Loud…

Learning happens with **Frequency**, **Intensity** and **Repetition**. So, this week, repeat these declarations loudly to yourself in front of a mirror at least 6 times daily.

❖ I want to be remembered as a person who was a carrier of a pioneering spirit amidst crisis.

❖ I will defy all odds and look forward with boldness and audacity.

❖ I will place these moments of crisis in perspective so I can experience the full enjoyment of life and its challenges.

[Chapter 3]

MENTAL AGILITY

Kelvin McCree

*"You are today where your thoughts have brought you;
you will be tomorrow where your thoughts take you."*
—James Allen

IN A SURVEY conducted by My Protein covering 1,350 Americans aged 18 to 65, it was discovered that the average American adult spends $155 per month on their health and fitness.[12] In case you haven't added that up, that's an average of $112,000 in their lifetime!

No one can argue against the motto that "health is wealth," but what is a life that is physically fit, yet unable to mentally face life's constant challenges. Fitness is often centered around the body and making physical changes, with the mental exhilaration that follows a workout. However, our brains are just like every other tissue and benefits from receiving exercise.

What exactly is mental agility?
    Why is developing mental agility important?

What motivates us to incorporate mental agility into our lives?

Mental agility is about our ability to alter our direction, mentally manage change, and adjust mindsets to operate successfully.

Mental agility allows our thoughts to be fluid during change moments. Being mentally agile is a challenge everyone should embrace. With the change and velocity of disruption, it is essential to our mental peace.

For us to be mentally agile, we need to focus on mindsets not just skill sets. Why? Because mindsets will determine the pace at which the change takes place.

Mindsets are our mental lenses that orient us toward a unique way of understanding an experience. Mindsets also guide us toward corresponding actions and responses. Mindsets drive our thinking, learning, behavior, and ultimately, determine the lenses by which we view change.

There are many wonderful examples of people who have used mental agility to manage change. One such person is portrayed in my all-time favorite movie, "In Pursuit of Happiness." Life is a struggle for Chris Gardner, who ends up a single parent, evicted from his apartment, and he and his young son find themselves alone with no place to go. Even though Chris eventually lands a job as an intern at a prestigious brokerage firm, the position pays no money. He and his young son end up living in shelters and having to endure many hardships.

Time after time, Chris masters his emotions and comes up gracious and smiling after being dealt a serious blow and was often able to go back to the people involved and create an opportunity for himself.

Even after getting what he perceived would make him happy, he still had to face change! Through it all, Chris refuses to give in to despair. With a focus on overcoming the disruption he faced, he created a better life for himself and his son and ultimately, adapted to find success.

> "The future was uncertain, absolutely, and there were many hurdles, twists, and turns to come, but as long as I kept moving forward, one foot in front of the other, the voices of fear and shame, the messages from those who wanted me to believe that I wasn't good enough, would be stilled." – Chris Gardner.[13]

Adapt or Perish

Benjamin Vickers, a baker in the city where I live, shared a motto with me he stated his family has had over several generations. It has proven to be sage advice for life's disruption. Benjamin says he has been using this old family motto to keep his downtown Lakeland bakeshop a float during the COVID-19 pandemic which simply says, *You adapt or perish.* The "adapt or perish" motto was borne from his family's survival of Nazi Germany's invasion of Poland nearly 80 years ago where, Poland lost 66,000 citizens, almost 134,000 wounded, and 694,000 captured.

Because of the sage advice of "adapt or perish," Benjamin has not only survived the current disruption, but is flexing his innovative skills to adapt to the changing state and expand his business.

John F. Kennedy once said, "There's only one unchangeable truth and that is, everything will change."[14]

> *Does this statement sound like your life now or something you've thought at some point, "Things didn't quite go as I planned?"*

Describe your reaction:

_____

_____

_____

Developing Mental Agility

> *So how do we develop Mental Agility?*
> *What is the anchor that fosters our ability to be mentally agile?*

Mental Agility begins and is anchored by a Growth Mindset. A growth mindset is the belief that I can change my talents, abilities, and intelligence. This differs from a fixed mindset, which is the belief that I cannot change these key attributes. The growth mindset is a priority and it influences how we navigate unfamiliar thresholds.

People who tend to function with a fixed mindset tend to: prioritize looking good, validation, and do not believe they can improve their emotional intelligence, talents, or abilities. Another key distinction between growth mindsets and fixed mindsets is the latter seeks to avoid failure or any hint they have failed.

Growth mindset says I possess the talent, ability, and intelligence to navigate this or **I can learn and grow**! Disruption for them, therefore, is a growth opportunity.

**Growth Mindset = Mental Agility
and makes us far more adaptable to change.**

Highlight the phrases that apply to your mindset.

- ❖ I believe can change my abilities in the face of crisis.

- ❖ I prioritize looking good.

- ❖ I believe I can continually improve my intelligence.

- ❖ I look for validation from others.

- ❖ I do not believe I can improve my talents.

- ❖ I cannot adjust my emotional intelligence.

- ❖ I am limited by my abilities.

Recognizing Resistance

Princeton Research has shown: "When the brain is in the midst of worry and uncertainty, the brain slows down. When the brain slows down and experiences worry, it no longer produces neurogenesis which is the process of growing neurons which grows the brain. If the brain slows down because of worry, it struggles with creativity. Secondly, worry is a producer of stress. Thirdly, stress is directly linked to fear. When worry, stress, and fear are functioning, they slow down the brain's operating system. What does this all mean? **It suggests that our resistance to change slows down our brains operating system, we're no longer innovating during change and worse, not growing at the rate we could.**[15]

The stark truth is, we cannot develop mental agility when we resist change.

We know when we are resisting change when:

- Falling back into old ways of thinking is a sign of change resistance or survival instincts.

- No longer asking, "How can I grow from this," indicates you are resisting change.

To overcome this resistance, I encourage you to take three important steps.

1. Be aware of the mindset that is conducive to mental agility.

2. Be aware of your mindset in relation to mental agility.

3. Focus on getting 1 percent better in your mental agility each day.

Pause and Reflect…

Based on what you learned in this chapter, you should now be able to answer these questions posed at the beginning of the chapter:

- *What exactly is mental agility?*

- *Why is developing mental agility important?*

- *What motivates us to incorporate mental agility into our lives?*

- *So how do we develop Mental Agility?*

- *What is the anchor that foster our ability to be mentally agile?*

If you could focus on these simple steps, where would you be in one year?

1. Be aware of the mindset that is conducive to mental agility.

2. Be aware of your mindset in relation to mental agility.

3. Focus on getting 1 percent better in your mental agility each day.

Review the Key Points highlighted in this chapter. Journal what revelation you received from each one and how it will affect how you look at and deal with change and disruptions in your life.

➤ Mental agility is about our ability to alter our direction, mentally manage change, and adjust mindsets to operate successfully.

➤ Time after time, Chris masters his emotions and comes up gracious and smiling after being dealt a serious blow and was often able to go back to the people involved and create an opportunity for himself.

➤ It suggests that our resistance to change slows down our brains operating system, we're no longer innovating during change and worse, not growing at the rate we could.

Say Out Loud...

Learning happens with **Frequency, Intensity** and **Repetition**. So, this week, repeat these declarations loudly to yourself in front of a mirror at least 6 times daily.

❖ I believe can change my abilities in the face of crisis.

❖ I believe I can continually improve my intelligence.

❖ I believe I can improve my talents.

[Chapter 4]

VICTIM OR VICTOR

Mercidieu Phillips

*"The victim mindset dilutes the human potential.
By not accepting personal responsibility for our
circumstances,
we greatly reduce our power to change them."*
—Steve Maraboli[16]

LIFE, AS AN ever-fleeting reality, gives all of us a fair chance at some common experiences. There is no one who has graced this planet as a human being who can exclusively claim a pain-free life.

Crisis and traumatic moments are equal-opportunity visitors.

The notion that someone is without any tangible and visible evidence of a certain degree to of unforeseen trauma and disruptive moments is false. It is in fact a fallacious belief to patronize if one ventures to allow the mind to be void of just how difficult this experience known as life can be. The challenge now is not so much in the already aforementioned truth, but how one navigates this reality and come out as a victor rather than a victim.

Slipping into the always open grip of victimhood is indeed an option that pops up on the crowded menu options of your life's dashboard. Deciding to engage in a space complete with the thoughts, feelings, and behaviors of a victim is always a personal choice. While there may be very creative ways at attempting to transfer the blame and provide superficially, justifiable reasons for such option, it remains a wanted selection. A crisis contains several critical elements from which the person experiencing it must choose. Let's take a deeper look into some of the elements that constitutes both a victim and a victor.

Elements of Victimhood

Blame:

The blame game is the most popular non-contact sport. It boasts a roster that is full and always at work. This game has very few rules and the referee is often the player in the game. Blaming an event or occurrence is an historic and popular human activity. From the time, a child is able to engage in mischievous act to the time when they are back to child-like status in a nursing home, human beings are pre-wired by nature to always deflect responsibility for their participation in a particular reality.

The global pandemic that is COVID19 has resurrected all the once low-lying skeptics and conspiracy theorist. Those who willingly traffic in the pointless activity of blaming governments and world leaders have been handed fresh fuel to energize their raging anger against virtually all forms of institutionalized order. They are the fringe patronizing proponents of debunked theories and unfounded rhetoric. Why do they do this you may ask? There answer to such question would most likely require an entire other book co-written with a psychologist or one whose job is to interpret behaviors for the benefit of the one behaving and those observing.

Then, there are those who look inward and blame themselves as the magnet that has attracted such misfortune. These people tend to look deep into their past to find traces of "karma" inducing behaviors. They often think that this current situation is payback for something done in the past that is now violently catching up to them. Not only is it counterproductive to venture into this type of activity, it is also very dangerous to the welfare of the one thinking this way and those closely associated with such thinking! Assaulting self is never the needed solution in a crisis.

The blame game is not the antidote that will reality alleviate the anguish or lessen the sting of the moment.

The conversation about the spiritual aspects of a crisis can range from the super religious fanatics who attribute everything that moves to a god or spiritual entity to those who are angry at "God" and blame Him for all evil experiences. It is both convenient and easy to go down this road for the simple fact that the gods being blamed usually don't produce a comeback.

Ask Yourself…

- *Have I engaged in the blame game to deflect responsibility for my participation in a specific reality?*

- *Have I blamed the COVID19 situation on governments and world leaders?*

- *Do I blame myself for a current crisis because of choices I have made in the past?*

- *Do I blame God for painful events in my life?*

- *Has blaming alleviated the anguish or lessen the sting of the moment?*

Idleness:

I grew up hearing my mom repeat a village proverb that says, "Work is liberty." I always wondered what she meant that one discovers freedom in work. I always saw work as something that you are forced to do instead of being able to play all day with my friends. This is until I became a pre-teen and was forced to begin my working career at the tender age of twelve. If the statement is true, that work is freedom, then we must consider the reverse of that same statement. Idleness is captivity! Crisis moments come as opportunities to settle for the reality of the present situation. These moments provide a seat at the table of nothingness and flashes the one-sided page of life's limited choices. The person who does not create an uncomfortable seating position by laying down tacks labeled with greatness and purpose before sitting will unwillingly recline in posture of failure.

Motivational speakers and leadership development guru Zig Ziglar once said that, "If you aim at nothing, you will hit it 100 percent of the time."[17]

Complacency is the birthplace of failure and idleness is a BFF of failure and a constant companion of limited advancement.

A powerful crisis met with a low expectation of self-reinforced by an attitude of complacency is the perfect mix to create a reality filled with frustration. The energy that takes you beyond the moment is the willingness to push past the pile of obstacles sitting by the roadside of life.

Boldness is the key to igniting the flame of a prosperous future.

Imagine the crisis you are facing is like walking into a room where you are surrounded by doors. These doors are labeled work, idleness, complacency, boldness, opportunity, and advancement.

- *Which door have you chosen in the past?*

- *Which door will bring you the success you seek in life?*

Associative Thinking:

"Misery loves company" is a phrase I'm sure you have heard repeated many times. When a crisis occurs, we usually default to the most comfortable act possible. For some, it comes in the form of developing new coping mechanisms like traveling on an adventurous journey to a place that is as far away as possible. I know an individual who was going through a very bitter separation from their spouse. This person's way of feeling better about the situation was to go on a seventeen-day vacation! After enjoying the privilege of experiencing three world-class resorts during this much needed getaway, I had a chance to chat with this person and to inquire about the experience. While it was great, I was told, the problem was a large credit card bill waiting in the mailbox and the problem had not moved one inch from where it stood prior to the trip.

A person engaging in associative thinking will usually find a group of like-minded friends or associates who will accept their choice to remain as is. This type of dysfunctional associative thinking creates the perfect environment to accommodate the accepted state of being. Associative thinking in this space is normally for the sake of maintenance rather than motion.

Have you chosen one of the elements of victimhood or are you ready to navigates this reality and come out as a victor rather than a victim?

Victors on Demand

Mindset:

The hardest part of living through a crisis is learning to beneficially use the moments to emerge with the rare prize of appreciative results. The emergence of victory or celebratory moments is not the work of an under thinker. It is not the display of unscarred hands, unscathed emotions, or countless sleepless nights. The strength of the victor is both seen and felt in the effortless movement of their being beyond the boundaries of the moment.

✓ Check off the mindsets that describe your approach to a crisis:

  o Allows defeat and failure to collapse before entry.

  o Facilitates the fascinating ballerina like motions of the delicate dance of tension and progress.

  o Stamps out the clumsy attempts of an incredible and possibly debilitating moment.

  o Places a crushing stranglehold around the neck of defeat and demands its exit from your sphere.

  o Learns how to successfully negotiate the competing forces of present reality and new possibilities.

  o Possesses the uncanny ability to visualize treasure in the midst of darkness.

While victors are the witnesses of crisis moments,

they control the variables by remaining the constant.

Resolve:

A crisis places everyone at the intersection of bold-ness and fear. The chaotic scene of a crisis is often the starting point of a long and arduous journey down into the abyss of despair or a steep and exhilarating climb towards the mountain top of victory.

The pleasure of an imagined picture of survival will at times serve as the weapon that allows the victor to firmly grip the sharp edges of the moment. The inner fortitude of the victor produces an ability to swiftly and decisively move around the concentric circle of trepida-tion, complacency, and skin-crawling fear.

Resolve is the distinctive factor that gives you the energy to fight off the real-life effects of the crisis.

A crisis can be draining and taxing on both the psyche as well as the physique. It is like that hose that attaches to your being and desires to suck the life out of you.

The forces of a crisis require the installation of "hur-ricane type" emotional windows that are designed to absorb the catastrophic effect of high impact winds. The resolve I speak of here, is the protective barrier that keeps the elements of the crisis in their proper place while shielding the victor from all intended effects.

Motion Driven:

The law of inertia also known as Newton's first law states the following, "A mass at rest tends to remain at rest; a mass moving at a constant velocity tends to keep moving at that velocity, unless acted upon by an outside force."[18] At this point, you are probably wondering what in the world does the law or principle of inertia have to do with a book about navigating through a crisis.

If you carefully inspect the premise of the law of inertia, you will soon discover that it is relevant to the discussion at hand.

- *See yourself as the mass at rest due to a situation or event that is not of your doing.*

- *You are going to be moved by the force of the crisis wrestling with your position.*

- *Now see the crisis as the mass moving at a constant velocity.*

- *You are the force that will need to act upon the moving force of the crisis!*

A crisis is **not invitation** to live in resignation or fear. While understanding and acknowledging the seriousness of a crisis, it should never become a crutch for the mind-bending decision to remain sterile. An unforeseen crisis encompasses the slowly developing power that could cripple anyone willing to give shelter to its presence.

The victor is a motion driven, forward-thinking and defeat defying individual who repeatedly refuses the popular position of "it what it is." It is at this place that the victor stands tall above all the other possibilities nestled in a crisis. This is where the ones who experience the same point of departure amidst the crisis to split into the direction of better or worse.

The remarkable outcomes will always be the visible manifestation of the unseen choice to navigate and not capitulate.

Closing Thought

Like everything else in life, a crisis has boundaries. As real and painful as a crisis may be, each crisis has a boundary. I began thinking about this concept as I reflected on a trip to Canada several years ago to fulfill a keynote address for a group of nonprofit organizations' annual gathering. I was in Boston Massachusetts the previous week and decided to drive to Canada rather than take the quick airplane ride. I wanted to experience what it was like to literally travel from one country to another by automobile.

As we approached the Canadian border, we had to stop to produce proper identification to the border patrol officer on duty. After verifying that we were legit, we were then asked to answer a series of question which also included things we promised not to engage in while visiting Canada. While our visit to the country was not prohibited, our behavior while there needed to show both understanding and respect for the law. Further, there was a time stamp on our entry card that alerted us of the permissible duration of our stay.

A crisis is a visitor in your territory, and you are the border patrol officer.

- 🖐 It is up to you to set the boundaries to govern its behavior.

- 🖐 If you allow it free reign and unlimited access to your being, it will take up as much mental and emotional real estate as possible.

- 🖐 If you fail to control its footprints on the soil of your soul, you will soon be trampled under its large feet as a suffocating victim.

- 🖐 You must put a time stamp on how long it stays and also how brief your visit to that place of despair will be.

Over history, the heroes of every crisis have been those who learned how to create boundaries for the unannounced visitor. The crisis knows no limit except those you set in place. It will demand more if requests are not vetted through the pre-disposed mind of the victor. However, if you decide to set the parameters of operation, you will enjoy the endless privileges of an unbridled victor.

🗝 *Pause and Reflect…*

A crisis contains several critical elements from which the person experiencing it must choose.

First, review the elements of **victimhood** as presented in this chapter.

Circle those you have found yourself choosing in a crisis situation.

Blame   **Idleness**   **Associative Thinking**

Now define:

The Mindset of a victor

_____

The Resolve of a victor

_____

What being Motion Driven means to a victor

_____

Which of these have you chosen when faced with a crisis situation?

Review the Key Points highlighted in this chapter. Journal what revelation you received from each one and how it will affect how you look at and deal with change and disruptions in your life.

> ➤ **Crisis and traumatic moments are equal-opportunity visitors.**

- ➤ The blame game is not the antidote that will alleviate the anguish or lessen the sting of the moment.

- ➤ Boldness is the key to igniting the flame of a prosperous future.

- ➤ Complacency is the birthplace of failure and idleness is a BFF of failure and a constant companion of limited advancement.

- ➤ While victors are the witnesses of crisis moments, they control the variables by remaining the constant.

- ➤ Resolve is the distinctive factor that gives you the energy to fight off the real-life effects of the crisis.

- ➤ The remarkable outcomes will always be the visible manifestation of the unseen choice to navigate and not capitulate.

Living the life of a victor in lieu of the burden-laden life of a victim is never accidental. It is always the result of rugged decisiveness over common convenience.

Nothing + Nothing = Nothing
No Decision + No Decision = No Decision

Continuation of a repetitive and predictable behavior provides the bitter and stale result of yesterday.

However, the modification of self, combined with the relentless pursuit of newness, always yields the delectable fruit of a broad horizon.

Say Out Loud...

Learning happens with **Frequency**, **Intensity** and **Repetition**. So, this week, repeat these declarations loudly to yourself in front of a mirror at least 6 times daily.

- ❖ **I choose not to continue repetitive and predictable behavior.**

- ❖ **I choose modification of self.**

- ❖ **I choose the relentless pursuit of newness.**

- ❖ **I choose to be a victor and not a victim even amid a crisis.**

[Chapter 5]

GAME-CHANGERS

Mercidieu Phillips

*"Transformational leaders don't start by denying the world around them.
Instead they describe a future they'd like to create instead."*
—Seth Godin[19]

THE ANNALS OF history are stuffed with individuals who have left an indelible mark on it. These change agents are pillars of courage and strength. They serve as historical pyramids for generation after generation. What an in-depth study of history provides is that, each epoch provides people who defy the odds, trample over obstacles, and rise up to meet each demand placed on them by their time. The common thread that binds all of these heroes together is usually a sense of calling. A calling to live exponentially and intentionally. This calling upends all personal ambitions, attempts at selfishness, and greed.

They answer to a voice that refuses to let them sit by and do nothing. They all exhibit an uncommon degree of resolve and conviction. Through their actions of bravery, some have left followable traces of determination, audacity, and shear grit. Others have moved their observers to tears, elevated purpose, and fostered life altering action.

The ink placed on sheets of paper chronicling the deeds of these people serves as marks of distinction rather than just "ink." While in their essential nature, they are just ordinary human beings much like the remainder of the human race, their being contains traits of purpose, power, and otherness.

The unprecedented offerings of this time in history demands the apparition of similar courageous game changers. The option of convenience has dissipated in value and is being forcibly replaced by urgency. A crisis or challenge always serves as a necessary set of needle-nosed pliers to pinch out the powerful abilities trapped between the crevices of can and cannot. These moments come as a heavy-duty tow truck dispatched to rescue purpose that has remained helplessly stranded by the roadside of success.

As previously mentioned, we, this current generation is very fortunate to have the life, leadership, and example of so many to follow. If I dared to list all of those who have at one time or another offered samples of change, this book would require the arms of more than one person to carry it and the eyeballs of so many to capture the abundance of information. Therefore, for the sake of just pricking your curiosity and hopefully igniting your own passion, the next few pages will be dedicated to closely, but partially examining the life and contributions of six people I deemed critical for the purpose stated: William Wilberforce, Dr. Martin Luther King Jr., Nelson Mandela, Mother Theresa, George W. Bush, and Steve Jobs.

The Reach of One Man

One of the greatest crises to ever visit the collective existence of humanity was the horrific practice of slavery that allowed various continents to thrive while destroying the dignity and decency of another group of people. It was one of the darkest periods in human history. Slavery was a pandemic of epic proportions. It was a crisis to anyone who ever owned a conscience beyond their own standard. Despite the darkness of the moment and the thickness of the reality, there were some whose sense of duty and moral obligation to a better world, could not leave them as mere bystanders. Since learning of this experience in my world history and civics courses, I have managed to develop a level of deep appreciation for the work of one of history's greatest and most recognized game-changers.

William Wilberforce (1759–1833) was a British politician, philanthropist, and a leader of the movement to abolish the slave trade in England. He began his political career in 1780, eventually becoming an independent Member of Parliament (MP) for Yorkshire from 1784 until 1812.

In 1785, he became an evangelical Christian, which resulted in major changes to his lifestyle. Wilberforce began to question whether he should remain in public life. He sought guidance from John Newton, a leading evangelical Anglican clergyman who was Rector of St. Mary Woolnoth in London. Newton and other evangelicals counseled him to remain in politics where he could introduce bills that could bring about social reform. He resolved to do so "with increased diligence and conscientiousness." He stayed true to that resolve to promote Christianity and Christian ethics in private and public life.

His life radically changed again when he came into contact with Thomas Clarkson and a group of anti-slave-trade activists in 1787. Clarkson encouraged Wilberforce to take on the cause of abolition and he soon became one of the leading English abolitionists. Wilberforce's involvement in the abolition movement was motivated by a desire to put his Christian principles into action and to serve God in public life. He and other evangelicals were horrified by what they saw as a depraved and un-Christian trade, motivated by the greed and avarice of the slave owners and traders.

Wilberforce sensed a call from God, writing in his journal in 1787, "God Almighty has set before me two great objectives, the suppression of the Slave Trade and the Reformation of Manners [moral values]."

Despite the decreased interest in abolition during the French Revolution, Wilberforce continued to diligently introduce abolition bills throughout the 1790s.

William Wilberforce gave the following speech before the House of Commons on April 18, 1791:[20]

Let us not despair; it is a blessed cause, and success, ere long, will crown our exertions. Already we have gained one victory; we have obtained the recognition of their human nature, which, for a while was most shamefully denied. This is the first fruits of our efforts; let us persevere and our triumph will be complete. Never, never will we desist till we have wiped away this scandal from the Christian name, released ourselves from the load of guilt, under which we at present labour, and extinguished every trace of this bloody traffic, of which our posterity, looking back to the history of these enlightened times, will scarce believe that it has suffered to exist so long a disgrace and dishonour to this country.

William Wilberforce headed the parliamentary campaign against the British slave trade for twenty years until the passage of the <u>Slave Trade Act of 1807</u>. The lessons left on the table of change by Wilberforce are abundant. They are deep, thought-provoking, and demand a response. The narrative shared about the work this game-changer engaged in is meant to awaken a like-minded sense of resolve as you interact with the words carefully placed on these pages you hold in your hand. What can we learn from Wilberforce and apply in our lives?

- *Strong conviction requires a corresponding action.* Wilberforce's conviction compelled him to act even when political, social, and economic forces strongly opposed him. Belief is more than mental assent or a stated position about an issue or crisis. Belief that births conviction must move us to "do the right thing" regardless of the cost.

- *Game Changers persist and never quit in the pursuit of righteousness and justice.* To right wrongs requires diligent, persistent action over extended periods of time. Instant and quick solutions never work. Each game changer we are overviewing in this part of my survey, spent years and even decades to effect change.

- *Change requires a huge investment of time, work, and focus.* A friend of mine teaches that change requires that we…

  - Focus

  - Fight

  - Finish

As you read on, keep these three imperatives for change in mind. In working for change in your personal life, professional career, or in the public arena, strive to avoid the appetizing bait of distraction. Develop a destiny promoting discipline and don't let anything or anyone distract you from your laser focus. Fight through opposition from unforeseen moments, determined enemies, and well-intentioned friends who fear change. Finally, finish the work, navigate the challenge, decide tomorrow's reality now…stop procrastinating.

A Moral Force

As I am actively writing this chapter, our country, the United States of America and several parts of the world are deeply embroiled in the issue of social justice. The recent high-profile deaths of African Americans as a result of police brutality and the experience of an adversely tilted justice system have created a re-visitation of ghosts that we all thought were buried a long time ago. An old game has suddenly changed and is in search of courageous participants, game-changers.

Game changers are those who take notice of an opportunity to impact a moment. They are the ones who refuse to make an agreement or sign an accord with complacency or passivity. The recent protests and civil unrest added to the ferocious spread of COVID19, have created a new reality that demands a look into the annals of history to analyze and learn from past game-changers. A thorough exercise in this arena can never happen without stopping in the history marker set by a leader who responded to a crisis during his time and in which we still find both the dark stain of hurt and the bright light of potential.

Dr. Martin Luther King (1929–1968) was an African American minister and activist who became the most visible spokesperson and leader in the civil rights movement from 1955 until his assassination in 1968. King is best known for advancing civil rights through non-violence and civil disobedience. His form of leadership was inspired by his Christian beliefs and the nonviolent activism of Mahatma Gandhi. Dr. King demonstrated the characteristics of a game-changer in the way he navigated a volatile situation and crisis. His commanding presence fueled by a deep sense of moral obligation served as pillars that girded his forward movement and history-altering efforts.

Dr. King led the 1955 Montgomery bus boycott that lasted for 385 days. The situation became so tense during the boycott that King's house was bombed. However, King's role in the bus boycott transformed him into a national figure.

In 1957, Dr. King, Ralph Abernathy, Fred Shuttlesworth, Joseph Lowery, and other civil rights activists founded the Southern Christian Leadership Conference (SCLC). The group was created to coordinate the moral authority and organize the power of black churches to conduct nonviolent protests in the service of civil rights reform. The group was inspired by the crusades of evangelist Billy Graham, who befriended King. King led the SCLC until his death.

Dr. King also helped organize the nonviolent 1963 protests in Birmingham, Alabama, and the March on Washington, where he delivered his famous, "I Have a Dream" speech on the steps of the Lincoln Memorial.

The 1963 March on Washington made specific demands: an end to racial segregation in public schools; meaningful civil rights legislation, including a law prohibiting racial discrimination in employment; protection of civil rights workers from police brutality; a $2 minimum wage for all workers (equivalent to $17 in 2019);

and self-government for Washington, D.C., which was governed by congressional committee at that time.

Despite tensions, the march was a resounding success. More than a quarter of a million people of diverse ethnicities attended the event, sprawling from the steps of the Lincoln Memorial onto the National Mall and around the reflecting pool. At the time, it was the largest gathering of protesters in Washington, D.C.›s history.

Global recognition of this game-changer reached a high point when on October 14, 1964, King won the Nobel Peace Prize for combating racial inequality through nonviolent resistance. Dr. King believed that organized, nonviolent protests against the system of southern segregation known as the Jim Crow laws would lead to extensive media coverage of the struggle for black equality and voting rights. Journalistic accounts and televised footage of the daily deprivation and indignities suffered by Southern blacks, and the segregationist violence and harassment of civil rights workers and marchers, produced a wave of sympathetic public opinion that convinced the majority of Americans that the civil rights movement was the most important issue in American politics in the early 1960s.

Dr. King and the SCLC put into practice many of the principles of those who preferred to have a different approach and applied the tactics of nonviolent protest with great success by strategically choosing the method of protest and the places in which protests were carried out. King was criticized by other black leaders during the course of his participation in the civil rights movement because of this nonviolent approach. As a disciplined game-changer, he refused the temptation to divert from what he knew would be effective in the long term. His unique ability to effect change in a moment when change was desperately needed provided a template for all who dare embrace the significance of a moment to take its possibilities past the present reality.

The Civil Rights Act was enacted in 1964 due to the relentless efforts, courageous tenacity, and transformational leadership of Dr. Martin Luther King Jr.[21] What are the irrefutable lessons of crisis navigation can we learn from King's leadership:

- *Vision trumps opposition.* In the pursuit of change, game-changers must always remember the power of focusing on the possibilities and less on the obstacles. Having a clear vision as a companion during a crisis provides the life raft one needs to successfully swim through the rip currents of fear.

- *Go beyond the moment.* All talk may tickle the ears of those around you, but motivational speeches only rally support…more is required. Yes, Dr. King was a powerful speaker, preacher, and writer. However, he moved beyond a moment of inspiration to implementation. Pursued by committed change agents, also known as game-changers, change brings lasting results.

- *Change the narrative.* Game-changers recognize a reality and immediately seek ways to redirect it. A giant such as Dr. King managed to change the narrative from what was happening to why it was morally unfitting for a nation whose foundations rested on something higher than its current practices or culture. He changed the conversation from people to human beings.

A Giant of History

Much like a good master of ceremony creatively introduces an audience to a keynote speaker or featured performer, moments introduce us to history and its treasure trove of valuable lessons. The annals of history are stuffed with the contributions of those who embraced an opportunity to leave an indelible mark on the fabric of society. The hall of fame of game-changers could never be complete without the transformational work of a man who risked it all just to see the concept of fairness and equality become a shared experience.

Nelson Mandela (1918 –2013) was a South African anti-apartheid revolutionary, political leader, and philanthropist who served as President of South Africa from 1994 to 1999. He was the country›s first black head of state and the first elected in a fully representative democratic election. His government focused on dismantling the legacy of apartheid by tackling institutionalized racism and fostering racial reconciliation. Ideologically an African nationalist and socialist, he served as the president of the African National Congress (ANC) party from 1991 to 1997.

After the National Party's white-only government established apartheid, a system of racial segregation that privileged whites, he and the ANC committed themselves to its overthrow. Although initially committed to non-violent protest, in association with the SACP, he led a sabotage campaign against the government. He was arrested and imprisoned in 1962, and subsequently sentenced to life imprisonment for conspiring to overthrow the state following the Rivonia Trial.

Mandela served 27 years in prison, split between Robben Island, Pollsmoor Prison, and Victor Verster Prison. Amid growing domestic and international pressure and with fears of a racial civil war, President F. W. de Klerk released him in 1990. Mandela and de Klerk led efforts to negotiate an end to apartheid, which resulted in the 1994 multiracial general election in which Mandela led the ANC to victory and became president.

Leading a broad coalition government which promulgated a new constitution, Mandela emphasized reconciliation between the country's racial groups and created the Truth and Reconciliation Commission to investigate past human rights abuses.

Widely regarded as an icon of democracy and social justice, he received more than 250 honors, including the Nobel Peace Prize. He is held in deep respect within South Africa and is often described as the "Father of the Nation."

"Gracious but steely, [Mandela] steered a country in turmoil toward a negotiated settlement: a country that days before its first democratic election remained violent, driven by divisive views and personalities. He endorsed national reconciliation, an idea he did not merely foster in the abstract but performed with panache and conviction in reaching out to former adversaries. He initiated an era of hope that, while not long-lasting, was nevertheless decisive, and he garnered the highest international recognition and affection." —Rita Barnard, *The Cambridge Companion*

His intellect was bolstered by a deep sense of calling and purpose. He once stated, "I have fought against white domination, and I have fought against black domination. I have cherished the ideal of a democratic and free society in which all persons will live together in harmony and with equal opportunities. It is an ideal which I hope to live for and to see realized. But if it needs be, it is an ideal for which I am prepared to die." —*Mandela's* Rivonia Trial Speech, *1964*

The answers to questions about his game-changer attitude produced more questions for the questioner than the original questions itself. Here is a brief example of this truth. "A friend once asked me how I could reconcile my creed of African nationalism with a belief in dialectical materialism. For me, there was no contradiction. I was first and foremost an African nationalist fighting for our emancipation from minority rule and the right to control our own destiny. But at the same time, South Africa and the African continent were part of the larger world. Our problems, while distinctive and special, were not unique, and a philosophy that placed those problems in an international and historical context of the greater world and the course of history was valuable. I was prepared to use whatever means necessary to speed up the erasure of human prejudice and the end of chauvinistic and violent nationalism." – Nelson Mandela, 1994

Mandela was widely considered a charismatic leader, described by biographer Mary Benson as, «a born mass leader who could not help magnetizing people.» He typically spoke slowly and carefully chose his words. Although he was not considered a great orator, his speeches conveyed «his personal commitment, charm and humor.»

Constantly polite and courteous, he was attentive to all, irrespective of their age or status, and often talked to children or servants. He was known for his ability to find common ground with very different communities. In later life, he always looked for the best in people, even defending political opponents to his allies, who sometimes thought him too trusting of others.

"Mandela can be considered in two related ways. First, he has provided through his personal presence as a benign and honest conviction politician, skilled at exerting power but not obsessed with it to the point of view of excluding principles, a man who struggled to display respect to all ... Second, in so doing he was able to be a hero and a symbol to an array of otherwise unlikely mates through his ability, like all brilliant nationalist politicians, to speak to very different audiences effectively at once." – Bill Freund

"I was not a messiah, but an ordinary man who had become a leader because of extraordinary circumstances." Boehmer described him as "a totem of the totemic values of our age: toleration and liberal democracy" and "a universal symbol of social justice."[22]

From Mandela's leadership, we can be inspired to…

- *Never quit.* Imagine being unjustly imprisoned for twenty-seven years. What can a person do from prison? Change a nation. Mandela continued to communicate his message of freedom and justice from within the most restrictive circumstances. He always found a way. He never gave up or quit.

- *Step out of preference and into conviction.* True conviction stays the course, pays the price, and pushes through the pain. Mandela's conviction came at great effort and cost to himself, his friends, and his family. His conviction did not cause him to disrespect others. We can disagree without damaging property or lives. Our vocal opposition cannot embrace violence or destruction. We cannot justify the end by choosing means that murder, destroy, or disgrace others. Conviction does not act upon what we believe but who we believe—the Prince of Peace.

- *Embrace courage for a courageous outcome.* Courage and boldness are required in the face of overwhelming crises. Courage refuses to allow fear to ever gain the upper hand. Boldness turns the doorknob of impossibilities and opens the door for the game-changer who is willing to make their way to an alternative experience.

An Advocate of Humanity

So far, I have intentionally tried to offer to you a mosaic of game-changers, ranging from those who successfully fought slavery, civil rights, and oppression of others.

There is one game-changer that I could not resist studying and presenting for the purpose of a balanced understanding of how crisis moments can often come masked in different forms. There are those who's call is to speak truth to power, some are assigned the role of activism, and then there are those whose activities simply require the tools of compassion and mercy. The following is a brief glimpse into the life and work of one of the world's most powerful women.

Mother Mary Teresa Bojaxhiu (1910–1997) left home in 1928 at the age eighteen to join the Sisters of Loreto at Loreto Abbey in Rathfarnham, Ireland, to learn English with the view of becoming a missionary. English was the language of instruction of the Sisters of Loreto in India. She arrived in India in 1929 and took her solemn vows in 1937 while she was a teacher at the Loreto convent school in Entally, eastern Calcutta. She served there for nearly twenty years and was appointed its headmistress in 1944. Although Teresa enjoyed teaching at the school, she became increasingly disturbed by the poverty surrounding her in Calcutta.

On September 10, 1946, Teresa experienced what she later described as "the call within the call." "I was to leave the convent and help the poor while living among them. It was an order. To fail would have been to break the faith." She began missionary work with the poor in 1948, replacing her traditional Loreto habit with a simple, white cotton sari with a blue border.

Teresa adopted Indian citizenship, spent several months in Patna to receive basic medical training at Holy Family Hospital, and then ventured into the slums. At the beginning of 1949, Teresa was joined in her effort by a group of young women and she laid the foundation for a new religious community helping the «poorest among the poor.»

Her efforts quickly caught the attention of Indian officials, including the prime minister.

"Our Lord wants me to be a free nun covered with the poverty of the cross. Today, I learned a good lesson. The poverty of the poor must be so hard for them. While looking for a home I walked and walked till my arms and legs ached. I thought how much they must ache in body and soul, looking for a home, food and health."

In 1950, Teresa received Vatican permission for the diocesan congregation that would become the Missionaries of Charity. In her words, it would care for «the hungry, the naked, the homeless, the crippled, the blind, the lepers, all those people who feel unwanted, unloved, uncared for throughout society, people that have become a burden to the society and are shunned by everyone.»

In 1952, Teresa opened her first hospice center with help from Calcutta officials. She converted an abandoned Hindu temple into the Kalighat Home for the Dying, free for the poor. Those brought to the home received medical attention and the opportunity to die with dignity in accordance with their faith. "A beautiful death," Teresa said, "is for people who lived like animals to die like angels—loved and wanted."

She opened a hospice for those with leprosy and established leprosy-outreach clinics throughout Calcutta, providing medication, dressings, and food. The Missionaries of Charity took in an increasing number of homeless children, so in 1955, Teresa opened the Children's Home of the Immaculate Heart, as a haven for orphans and homeless youth.

By 1997, the thirteen-member Calcutta congregation had grown to more than 4,000 sisters who managed orphanages, AIDS hospices and charity centers worldwide, caring for refugees, the blind, disabled, aged, alcoholics, the poor and homeless, and victims of floods, epidemics, and famine. By 2007, the Missionaries of Charity numbered about 450 brothers and 5,000 sisters worldwide, operating 600 missions, schools, and shelters in 120 countries.[23]

We might best learn how to lead and accomplish great things from a famous quote by Mother Teresa:

> *"People are often unreasonable and self-centered. Forgive them anyway.*
>
> *"If you are kind, people may accuse you of ulterior motives. Be kind anyway."*
>
> *"If you are honest, people may cheat you. Be honest anyway."*
>
> *"If you find happiness, people may be jealous. Be happy anyway."*

"The good you do today may be forgotten tomorrow. Do good anyway." "Give the world the best you have, and it may never be enough. Give your best anyway."

"For you see in the end, it is between you and God. It never was between you and them anyway." –Mother Teresa

Courage in an Age of Evil

In a previous section of this work, I briefly mentioned the event of September 11, 2001, and how that moment shook the foundation of the United States of America and re-shaped the way the world operates. In the midst of all the fracas and uproar, there was a single leader whose moment to lead was neither scripted nor predicted. After a bitter and hotly contested domestic electoral process, this leader would be thrust into a moment never seen before. His leadership and sense of duty have landed his work on these pages for your review.

George Walker Bush (1946) served as the 43rd president of the United States from 2001 to 2009. In response to the September 11 terrorist attacks, Bush created the United States Department of Homeland Security and launched a «War on Terror." The September 11 terrorist attacks were a major turning point in Bush's presidency. That evening, he addressed the nation from the Oval Office, promising a strong response to the attacks. He also emphasized the need for the nation to come together and comfort the families of the victims. Three days after the attacks, Bush visited Ground Zero and met with Mayor Rudy Giuliani, firefighters, police officers, and volunteers. Bush addressed the gathering via a megaphone while standing in a heap of rubble: "I can hear you. The rest of the world hears you. And the people who knocked these buildings down will hear all of us soon."

In a September 20 speech, Bush condemned Osama bin Laden and his organization Al-Qaeda, and issued an ultimatum to the Taliban regime in Afghanistan, where bin Laden was operating, to "hand over the terrorists, or ... share in their fate."

After September 11, Bush announced a global War on Terror. In his January 29, 2002 State of the Union Address, he asserted that an "axis of evil" consisting of North Korea, Iran, and Iraq was "arming to threaten the peace of the world" and "pose[d] a grave and growing danger."

The September 11 attacks (often referred to as **9/11**) were a series of four coordinated terrorist attacks by the Islamic terrorist group al-Qaeda against the United States on the morning of Tuesday, September 11, 2001. The attacks resulted in 2,977 fatalities, over 25,000 injuries, and substantial long-term health consequences, in addition to at least $10 billion in infrastructure and property damage. 9/11 is the single deadliest terrorist attack in human history and the single deadliest incident for firefighters and law enforcement officers in the history of the United States, with 343 and 72 killed, respectively.

Four passenger airliners which had departed from airports in the northeastern United States bound for

California were hijacked by nineteen al-Qaeda terrorists. Two of the planes, American Airlines Flight 11 and United Airlines Flight 175, crashed into the North and South towers, respectively, of the World Trade Center complex in Lower Manhattan. Within an hour and 42 minutes, both 110-story towers collapsed. Debris and the resulting fires caused a partial or complete collapse of all other buildings in the World Trade Center complex, including the 47-story 7 World Trade Center tower, as well as significant damage to ten other large surrounding structures. A third plane, American Airlines Flight 77, was crashed into the Pentagon (the headquarters of the U.S. Department of Defense) in Arlington County, Virginia, which led to a partial collapse of the building's west side. The fourth plane, United Airlines Flight 93, was initially flown toward Washington, D.C., but crashed into a field in Stonycreek Township, Pennsylvania, after passengers thwarted the hijackers.

Many countries strengthened their anti-terrorism legislation and expanded the powers of law enforcement and intelligence agencies to prevent terrorist attacks.

The destruction of the World Trade Center and nearby infrastructure seriously harmed the economy of New York City and had a significant effect on global markets. Wall Street was closed until September 17, and the U.S. and Canadian civilian airspaces until September 13. Many closings, evacuations, and cancellations followed, out of respect or fear of further attacks.

The attacks had a significant economic impact on United States and world markets. By the end of the week, the

DJIA had fallen 1,369.7 points (14.3%), at the time its largest one-week point drop in history. In 2001 dollars, U.S. stocks lost $1.4 trillion in valuation for the week.

In New York City, about 430,000 job-months and $2.8 billion in wages were lost in the first three months after the attacks. The economic effects were mainly on the economy's export sectors. Also hurt were small businesses in Lower Manhattan near the World Trade Center, 18,000 of which were destroyed or displaced, resulting in lost jobs and their consequent wages.

North American air space was closed for several days after the attacks and air travel decreased upon its reopening, leading to a nearly 20% cutback in air travel capacity, and exacerbating financial problems in the struggling U.S. airline industry.

The impact of 9/11 extends beyond geopolitics into society and culture in general. Immediate responses to 9/11 included a greater focus on home life and time spent with family, higher church attendance, and increased expressions of patriotism such as the flying of flags. 9/11 has also had a major impact on the religious faith of many individuals.

The Department of Homeland Security was created by the Homeland Security Act to coordinate domestic anti-terrorism efforts. The USA Patriot Act gave the federal government greater powers, including the authority to detain foreign terror suspects for a week without charge, to monitor telephone communications, e-mail, and Internet use by terror suspects, and to prosecute suspected terrorists without time restrictions. The

FAA ordered that airplane cockpits be reinforced to prevent terrorists from gaining control of planes, and assigned sky marshals to flights. Further, the Aviation and Transportation Security Act made the federal government, rather than airports, responsible for airport security. The law created the Transportation Security Administration to inspect passengers and luggage, causing long delays and concern over passenger privacy.[24]

What we can learn from President Bush might be summarized as:

- *Face Fear and Catastrophe with Resolve and Assertive Push-Back.* Terrorism in the forms of spiritual, emotional, mental, and physical abuse may be attacking you right now. Don't cower or run away. Get help! As a game-changer, you will need a team of supportive and equipped people to fight back. Get help! Ask for help! This moment was not designed to be experienced as a loner. It was not created for the use of your meager resources. As my colleague will share with you in a later chapter, relationships are the new economy. Let others in on your challenges and learn from them. President Bush used a powerful team to fight back…do the same.

- *Get up when others put you down.* Stop wallowing in self-pity. As I invited you in the previous chapter, choose to be a victor not a victim. You cannot fail if you refuse to quit.

A Global Disrupter

The entrance of COVID19 has forced the entire modern world to gain a deep appreciation for technology. The disruption caused by this pandemic has introduced scores of people to platforms and gadgets they never thought would be of much use to them. Every country in the world has either been touched or affected by the power of a simple word: Apple! It has often been said that behind every successful man is a powerful woman. The same can be said that behind every successful company or organization is a powerful leader. As we closely observe the epic rise of this amazing company, it is appropriate to take a closer look at the man who created this phenomenon in the midst of a critical moment in the information age.

Steven Paul Jobs (1955–2011) was an American business magnate, industrial designer, investor, and media proprietor. He was the chairman, chief executive officer (CEO), and co-founder of Apple Inc., the chairman and majority shareholder of Pixar, a member of The Walt Disney Company's board of directors following its acquisition of Pixar, and the founder, chairman, and CEO of NeXT. Jobs is widely recognized as a pioneer of the personal computer revolution of the 1970s and 1980s, along with Apple co-founder Steve Wozniak.

Jobs and Wozniak co-founded Apple in 1976 to sell Wozniak's Apple I personal computer. Together the duo gained fame and wealth a year later with the Apple II, one of the first highly successful mass-produced microcomputers. Jobs saw the commercial potential of the

Xerox Alto in 1979, which was mouse-driven and had a graphical user interface (GUI). This led to the development of the Macintosh in 1984, the first mass-produced computer with a GUI. The Macintosh introduced the desktop publishing industry in 1985 with the addition of the Apple LaserWriter, the first laser printer to feature vector graphics.

In 1985, Jobs founded NeXT, a computer platform development company that specialized in computers for higher-education and business markets. In addition, he helped to develop the visual effects industry when he funded the computer graphics division of George Lucas's Lucasfilm in 1986. The new company was Pixar, which produced the first 3D computer-animated feature film *Toy Story* (1995).

He worked closely with designer Jony Ive to develop a line of products that had larger cultural ramifications, beginning in 1997 with the «Think different" advertising campaign and leading to the iMac, iTunes, iTunes Store, Apple Store, iPod, iPhone, App Store, and the iPad. In 2001, the original Mac OS was replaced with a completely new Mac OS X, based on the NeXTSTEP platform, giving the OS a modern Unix-based foundation for the first time.

"Basically Steve Wozniak and I invented the Apple because we wanted a personal computer. Not only couldn›t we afford the computers that were on the market, those computers were impractical for us to use. We needed a Volkswagen. The Volkswagen isn't as fast or comfortable as other ways of traveling, but the VW owners can go where they want, when they want, and with whom they want. The VW owners have personal control of their car." – Steve Jobs

Scott McNealy, one of the cofounders of Sun Microsystems, said that Jobs broke a "glass age ceiling" in Silicon Valley because he'd created a very successful company at a young age.

"For what characterizes Apple is that its scientific staff always acted and performed like artists – in a field filled with dry personalities limited by the rational and binary worlds they inhabit, Apple's engineering teams had passion. They always believed that what they were doing was important and, most of all, fun. Working at Apple was never just a job; it was also a crusade, a mission, to bring better computer power to people. At its roots that attitude came from Steve Jobs. It was "Power to the People", the slogan of the sixties, rewritten in technology for the eighties and called Macintosh."–*Jeffrey S. Young, 1987. From the book, Steve Jobs: The Journey is the Reward (published 1988).*

In April 1977, Jobs and Wozniak introduced the Apple II and the Apple II became one of the first highly successful mass-produced microcomputer products in the world. Jobs was worth over $1 million in 1978 when he was just twenty-three years old. His net worth grew to over $250 million by the time he was twenty-five.

In 1983, Jobs lured John Sculley away from Pepsi-Cola to serve as Apple›s CEO, asking, «Do you want to spend the rest of your life selling sugared water, or do you want a chance to change the world?»

Jobs began directing the development of the Macintosh in 1981. On January 22, 1984, Apple aired a Super Bowl television commercial titled «1984" which ended with the words: "On January 24th, Apple Computer will introduce Macintosh. And you'll see why 1984 won't be like *1984.*"

In 1990, the NeXT workstation was known for its technical strengths, chief among them its object-oriented software development system. Jobs marketed NeXT products to the financial, scientific, and academic community, highlighting its innovative, experimental new technologies, such as the Mach kernel, the digital signal processor chip, and the built-in Ethernet port. Making use of a NeXT computer, English computer scientist Tim Berners-Lee invented the World Wide Web in 1990 at CERN in Switzerland.

Jobs touted it as the first "interpersonal" computer that would replace the personal computer. With its innovative NeXTMail multimedia email system, NeXTcube could share voice, image, graphics, and video in email for the first time. «Interpersonal computing is going to revolutionize human communications and groupwork,» Jobs told reporters.

He is listed as either primary inventor or co-inventor in 346 United States patents or patent applications related to a range of technologies from actual computer and portable devices to user interfaces (including touch-based), speakers, keyboards, power adapters, staircases, clasps, sleeves, lanyards, and packages.

iTunes is a media player, media library, online radio broadcaster, and mobile device management application developed by Apple. It is used to play, download, and organize digital audio and video (as well as other types of media available on the iTunes Store) on personal computers running the macOS and Microsoft Windows operating systems. The iTunes Store is also available on the iPod Touch, iPhone, and iPad. Through the iTunes Store, users can purchase and download music, music videos, television shows, audiobooks, podcasts, movies, and movie rentals in some countries, and ringtones, available on the iPhone and iPod Touch (fourth generation onward).

Apple began work on the first iPhone in 2005 and the first iPhone was released on June 29, 2007. The iPhone created such a sensation that a survey indicated six out of ten Americans were aware of its release. *Time* declared it «Invention of the Year» for 2007.

iPad is an iOS-based line of tablet computers designed and marketed by Apple. The first iPad was released on April 3, 2010; the most recent iPad models, the iPad (2017), iPad Pro, and iPad Mini 4, were released on September 9, 2015, and March 24, 2017. The user interface is built around the device›s multi-touch screen, including a virtual keyboard. The iPad includes built-in Wi-Fi and cellular connectivity on select models. As of April 2015, more than 250 million iPads have been sold.[25]

We must admit that the character and relational skills of Jobs could often be emotionally and psychologically abusive. We don't advocate that. But a "Do More" attitude marked Jobs' attitude—do more creatively, do more to capture the market in developing products that people need and will buy and use.

I encourage you to seize upon a "Do More" Attitude as powerfully described by John Mason:

- *Do More... Do more than exist—live.*

- *Do more than hear—listen.*

- *Do more than agree—cooperate.*

- *Do more than talk—communicate.*

- *Do more than grow—bloom.*

- *Do more than spend—invest.*

- *Do more than think—create.*

- *Do more than work—excel.*

- *Do more than share—give.*

- *Do more than decide—discern.*

- *Do more than consider—commit.*

- *Do more than forgive—forget.*

- *Do more than help—serve.*

- *Do more than coexist—reconcile.*

- *Do more than sing—worship.*

- *Do more than think—plan.*

- *Do more than dream—do.*

- *Do more than see—perceive. Do more than read—apply.*

- *Do more than receive—reciprocate.*

- *Do more than choose—focus.*

- *Do more than wish—believe.*

- *Do more than advise—help.*

- *Do more than speak—impart.*

- *Do more than encourage—inspire.*

- *Do more than add—multiply.*

- *Do more than change—improve.*

- *Do more than reach—stretch.*

- *Do more than ponder—pray.*

- *Do more than just live—live for Jesus.*

**—John Mason,
"You Can Do It—Even if Others Say You Can't"**

Before reading on, I want to ask you to pause and review what you have just learned from these amazing and inspiring leaders. Make a list of character qualities you want to develop within yourself and actions you need to take to improve and better not only yourself but the people and culture around you. Game changers see the opportunity that is nestled in the moment. They are the ones who will never accept the convenience offered by doubt or fear. Game changers challenge themselves and the ripple effect impacts others to challenge the cause before them. This moment of disruption is not intended to leave you without some tangible evidence of your careful and deliberate choice to enter the ranks of those who placed a marker on the boardwalk of history for others to use as a template towards greatness. The evidence of possibility is irrefutable. Now comes your decision to add to it or simply observe it…I humbly beg you to choose the former rather than the latter.

[Chapter 6]

CRYSTALIZING A CRISIS

Mercidieu Phillips

"In any moment of decision,
the best thing you can do is the right thing,
the next best thing is the wrong thing,
and the worst thing you can do is nothing."
—President Theodore Roosevelt[26]

WHEN HE WAS fired, it felt like his world was crashing in on him. With a wife at home and a family to take care, the announcement that his services were no longer needed came as a crushing blow. For a man who believed in working and taking responsibility, the loss of employment was indeed a very tough pill to swallow. Instead of taking the loss as a sign of defeat, he turned it into an opportunity to create a very successful business that is still prospering today.

In 1925, Howard Deering Johnson found a way to borrow $2,000.00 to acquire a small pharmacy in Wollaston, an unknown community in Quincy, Massachusetts. He sold everything from soda pop to ice cream. His entrepreneurial prowess led to the establishment of a sit-down restaurant. The success of his restaurants paved the way for entry into the hotel and lodging business.

In 1954, the company opened the first Howard Johnson's motor lodge in Savannah, Georgia. When Howard Johnson's Company went public in 1961, there were 605 restaurants, 265 company-owned and 340 franchised, as well as 88 franchised Howard Johnson's motor lodges in 32 states and the Bahamas.

By 1979, the "Host of the Highways" had become the largest hospitality company in America, with more than 1,000 restaurants and 500 motor lodges.[27] He created a brand that resonated with people and became recognizable to all who made travel and dining out a part of their lives. Whenever you see or visit a Howard Johnson hotel, you are witnessing the vision, determination, and ingenuity of a man who chose to use a difficult moment to create success.

Half Full or Half Empty?

Learning how to crystalize a crisis can be as taxing as it is exhilarating. The pressure of a crisis can be demoralizing or inspiring. The global crisis of COVID19 created an agenda with only two choices, fight or flee. It left the recipients with nothing more than the task of choosing to maximize the moment or allow the moment to maximize and exteriorize the predisposed fear lying dormant within.

There are those for whom this crisis has prompted the necessity to reconsider their career choices due to the downsizing of once thriving companies and organizations. The serious pullback of hesitant and fearful consumers have forced major corporations to strategically make cuts to long-tenured staffers. The pandemic is causing pandemonium on a wide scale level.

Small business owners are making creative shifts to survive the uncertainty of the times. There are also individuals who are planning to create a new business that is largely going to operate on an online platform. These are the people who refuse to lay down and allow the compact compressor known as COVID19 roll over them. They are rebelling against the convenience of the moment and striving for the greater things that will emerge out of this.

On the other hand, there are some who will see this as the proverbial apocalyptic moment that ushers them into total chaos and despair. These are the people who perpetually see the glass as half empty and make very little effort to move it passed that perceived line.

Cutting It Down to Size

How do you eat an elephant is the question that is often posed at the site of a seemingly unsurmountable issue? The answer is…you eat it one bite at a time. The first step to solving any problem is normalizing the scope by properly contextualizing the issue. The complexity and ferocious force of a crisis can clutter one's ability to decipher truth from fiction. This is why it is necessary to take a mental measuring tape to determine the exact dimensions of the crisis in order to create a feasible action plan.

Also, it is important to analyze the elements involved to engage the right set of tools as you trim the crisis to a manageable size. This may involve talking to someone else who may help provide some perspective on the issue. Engaging someone else can help make other unknown realities emerge and assist in tapering the waves of emotions that were set loose at the onset of the crisis.

Over the past few months, I have been involved in creating a community of people who find great solace in sharing their current mindset and the challenges they have had to face because of COVID19. These conversations and shared times have released the air out of the emotional blimp that otherwise would have lifted and carried them to an unwanted place. Freely sharing about a challenging situation is widely recommended by mental health experts.

Mike Urban, a clinical psychologist with Murphy, Urban and Associates, prefers the term physical distancing to social distancing. "When confronted with such enormous stress, we must rely on others for support," he said. "Physical distancing emphasizes the need to keep 6 to 10 feet apart and restrict activity outside of the home. Limit your sphere, but stay social in more creative ways," he says. He suggests reaching out to friends via FaceTime, Zoom, Snapchat "or even yelling across the alley to connect."[28]

Be creative and find ways to differentiate between social and physical distancing.

_____

_____

_____

Acquiring Fog Lights

I have the awesome privilege of living in the Sunshine State of Florida. We get to enjoy what is often referred to as year-round summer. Millions of people fly here from around the world to enjoy the great beaches and tropical weather. The great family amusement parks also make this a preferred destination when people are deciding where to go for that much needed relaxation time.

However, there are some mornings when the density of fog makes travel by car or an airplane really challenging. Due to my connection with several organizations in South Florida, I often have must make the drive from Southwest Florida where I live to the East coast, tri-county area.

During the mornings where the fog is very dense due to the Everglades, I need to use the fog light feature of the car while exercising great caution. I also use the windshield wipers to help keep my vision clear. Further, part of this careful approach sometimes requires that

I reduce my speed. The difference between when it is clear and foggy could easily be 45 minutes in travel time.

What is the point you may be asking? A crisis of any size can create a very foggy picture of what is ahead. It has the capacity to eliminate the unwanted elements blocking the limitless opportunities being hidden by the density of the fog. The fog lights I speak of here could be in the form of courses, webinars, books, new acquaintances, or even discovering a new passion.

Research courses and webinars that can help you prepare to continue moving forward in despite the fog created by a crisis. Journal what you discover and see if you acquire a new passion for adjusting to changes caused by the crisis.

_____

_____

_____

The decision to crystalize a crisis could simply mean adjusting your attitude from "settled" mode to open. It may require the acquisition of a new skill through training or certification program. In the same way that not all cars use the same size wiper blades to clear the windshield, everyone will not use the same methods or tools to gain proper perspective.

What is important is that you decide to find the "tools" that fit your unique situation.

New Skill:

_____

_____

New Method:

_____

_____

Innovation

Charles Darwin introduced us all to the theory known as the survival of this fittest. His basic premise was that life revolved around the idea that those who could fight through the toughest elements of life by constantly adapting to the current surroundings, were best positioned to survive. Innovation is extremely critical during this time.

The term innovation is defined as an action or process. It is best understood as the ability to create, develop, and foster a new thing or experience. As an executive coach and organizational consultant, I use this concept a lot when working with a businessperson or organizational leader when they are trying to find a new level of effectiveness that will improve the bottom line. We always begin by doing a deep dive into what they are currently doing.

The goal is to find what is working and why. Once we discover that, we move to what isn't working by taking a very objective look at all the factors that make up the company. It is always amazing to see the reaction of these brilliant leaders when we find things as simple as employee morale being a leading cause of success or failure. What is even more alarming is when we can find new money for the organization hidden in old and accepted habits. At the end of a deep dive, we normally try to come up with an "innovation plan" to correct what isn't working and to reinforce what is working.

At this point, you would probably want to pull out a legal note pad or a plain sheet of paper and make a list of all the activities you currently spend the most time on. This could be work, school, recreation, or anything you deem critical to your regular routine.

After you write everything down, divide the list into two categories: disposable, meaning I can do without and indispensable. Closely examine the two sides to determine where you will need to make major changes due to this disruption or crisis situation.

Keep in mind that real innovation is birthed in the cradle of brutal honesty. Its power is discovered through unmitigated boldness. The unseen gifts of a proportionate disruption are inconvenient displacement, soul chafing discomfort, and life altering decisions.

Innovation is a force that is unleashed when the straps of fear are removed and replaced with the combustible elements of courage and faith.

Successful people are usually known as great practitioners of turn around projects.

They are the ones who can take a setback and use it for a comeback.

✦ The factor of distinction for these people is simply-effort.

✦ Under the weight of a challenging moment, they find new ways to plunge ahead even if it means bearing the temporary scars of the left behind reality.

✦ They possess the ability to affect a common unwanted, unforeseen experience by employing the creative power of producing a new reality not readily seen by many.

While they do not dismiss the painful reality at hand, they find a way to lend a hand to their unstoppable future by vehemently refusing the temptation of commonality. Their actions are meant to violate the very boundaries being placed on them by the crisis. They are repeat offenders of the status quo as they find openings to a brighter and more promising future. Just enough is never good enough. They pedal through the difficult terrain of what is, in search of what can be. They are addicts of yes and staunch enemies of forced barriers fabricated by moments of disruption. This particular pedigree of people are not stragglers or paupers. They are tenacious, decisive, and daring. They consistently snatch victory from the menacing jaws of defeat.

These are the people who activate the truth of the Chinese proverb,
"A crisis is an opportunity riding a dangerous wind."

☞ *Pause and Reflect...*

This successful people club, though exclusive in nature, is also inclusive and is always accepting those who develop the required entry card of boldness.

Your exclusive membership invitation that has been delivered by this disruption or crisis patiently awaits.

Please RSVP now for a better tomorrow.

Review the Key Points highlighted in this chapter. Journal what revelation you received from each one and how it will affect how you look at and deal with change and disruptions in your life.

> ➢ **Research courses and webinars that can help you prepare to continue moving forward in spite of the fog created by a crisis.**

> ➢ **Innovation is a force that is unleashed when the straps of fear are removed and replaced with the combustible elements of courage and faith.**

> ➢ **These are the people who activate the truth of the Chinese proverb, "A crisis is an opportunity riding a dangerous wind."**

Say Out Loud...

Learning happens with **Frequency**, **Intensity** and **Repetition**. So, this week, repeat these declarations loudly to yourself in front of a mirror at least 6 times daily.

❖ I will be creative and find ways to differentiate between social and physical distancing.

❖ I will become a member of the successful people club.

❖ I will find new methods and tools to be successful even when facing a crisis situation.

[Chapter 7]

NOT LEAVING EMPTY HANDED

Kelvin McCree

"If a window of opportunity appears, don't pull down the shade."
—Tom Peters[29]

"Someone's sitting in the shade today because someone planted a tree a long time ago."
—Warren Buffet[30]

MANY PEOPLE WILL talk to you about success, but I've learned that it's just as important to talk about what usually happens first, FAILURE. Failure is always a demoralizing and upsetting experience.

**You cannot always control whether difficult things happen to you in life,
but you can control, to a large extent, how you react to them.**

Failure makes your mind trick you into believing things that aren't true. Unless you learn to respond to failures in psychologically adaptive ways, they will paralyze you, rob you of motivation, and limit your likelihood of success going forward.

Psychologically speaking, the most important thing to do after a failure is to understand its **impact** and how it affects your **thoughts, feelings**, and **behaviors.** Equally as important is substituting the term **failure** with the word, **feedback**. Feedback is defined as information about reactions to a product, a person's performance of a task, etc. which is used as a basis for improvement. It is a form of modification in order to improve something.

Substituting the word "feedback" for the word "failure"
allows us to focus on improvements and modifications instead of loss.

Perhaps you are familiar with the story of Orville and Wilbur Wright, also known as the Wright brothers. During their quest to build an airplane that had the ability for sustained flight, Orville's design only stayed up 12 seconds with a sustained height of 120 feet. On the other hand, Wilbur's design was able to have sustained flight for 60 seconds, reaching a height of 852 feet. The difference in both sustained time in the air and feet is remarkable, but what is often overlooked is they previously failed for two years and burned down a barn in the process.

The Feedback Lens

I believe Orville and Wilbur Wright did not view their mishaps as failure. Rather, they looked at the incidence through a Feedback Lens. This slight pivot in perspective takes us from "what happened to me" to "what can I learn from this?" In so doing, the moment transforms into an incubator for learning because survival that is not preceded by progressive action is nothing more than a prolonged crisis without a defined outcome.

Progressive Action:

> ✎ *Write a sentence describing a crisis that happened to you.*

> ✎ *Now reword this into what you learned from this experience.*

Another benefit of looking through the Feedback Lens is it keeps our hearts free from toxins that metastasize into progress polluters. Pollution affects the environment, our air quality, and has poisonous effects on life. While interpreting setbacks as simply failures, we introduce pollutants into our psychological environment and run the risk of leaving an experience empty handed. It is important to remember that in order get the most out of life's moments, we must internalize the goodness of life knowing that we can only give to others what is inside of us.

Once such example of this principle is Richard Montanez, an immigrant who dropped out of school in the fourth grade, leading to a series of low paying jobs from working in a slaughterhouse to washing cars. Eventually, he landed a job cleaning toilets at the Frito-Lay Rancho Cucamonga Plant in California which paid only $4 per hour. One day at the Frito Lay Plant he worked at, one of the machines processed thousands of bags of Cheetos without the cheese. After taking the cheese-less Cheetos home to his friends and family and incorporating flavors he learned growing up as an immigrant, Richard invented his own version of Cheetos. He wanted to pitch his idea to the then CEO, Roger Enrico. With his custom-designed packing and presentation that he developed in the local library, Richard boldly strolled into the office of the CEO and invented Flamin' Hot Cheetos. Well, the rest is history. Today, we know this invention as the Flamin' Hot Cheetos, Flamin' Hot Crunch, Flamin' Hot Puffs, and the list goes on. Richard is now a best-selling author, motivational speaker, and served as an Executive with the Pepsico Corporation.

There are moments in our lives we have misunderstood. Many of us have wrestled with capturing the breadth, width, and length of life and just when we thought we understood it, something happens to upset our clarity.

Progressive Action:

   📍 *As you look back at your own life and your journey, what can you discover and embrace?*

   📍 *Ask yourself, "How can I fine value and express the goodness stored within me with a life that is so unpredictable?"*

The question in life and business is not what happened, but what happened next.

What are you doing to overcome and ensure you don't come out of this empty-handed?

Pain-Based Decision-Making

Pain-based decision-making is defined as the central way you integrate your past into your present decisions.

Pain-based decisions are the opposite of values-based decisions.

Pain-Based Decision-Making entails three key dynamics:

- Your experiences lead you off the intended path of your life trajectory.

- You make unconscious and automatic choices based on your past.

- Your reaction to your past promotes an unhealthy interaction with your present.

Which of these have you experienced in your decision-making?
What was the outcome of that decision?

After encountering setbacks, disappointments, and loss, the one thing we all want is to get our lives back. The key to taking or getting our lives back is to begin vetting our decisions. This means having a set of values that you can refer to which may require taking a time out so you can vette your own heart.

Progressive Action:

🔎 *List the values you use to make an important decision.*

🔎 *Take a step back and considering how to handle your current crisis with values-based decisions instead of pain-based decisions.*

It is also important to become present not only **to the moment** but also **present to your internal reaction** to the moment. Pain-based decisions seek to ignore its affects while destroying the moment. Being present to the moment means not just being there, but being all there. In other words, consider the long-term effect of your decision.

There's a quote I once heard that says, "Chop wood, carry water" – in essence, it means don't chop would while carrying water and don't allow this to destroy either job.

Progressive Action:

🔎 *What is the long-term effect of the decision you are considering for handling your current crisis situation?*

Finally, discover the reason you choose to trust old patterns that have failed you repeatedly. Investing in patterns that have brought repeated challenges is a recipe for repeated failure. Seek to know why these old patterns empower you by identifying what was it you held onto.

Progressive Action:

🔎 Using the concepts of **cost, benefit, and analysis** to look at your relational landscape and ask yourself, what is this pain producing?

➢ Cost:

➢ Benefit:

➢ Analysis:

Reframing Me

Stress is a common emotion that confronts many of us. However, learning to reframe your mind is critical to minimizing your stress so that it doesn't adversely affect your relationships, basic decision making, or your overall peace. You live in a world of images and impressions and your whole life is an unfolding story. With each image, impression, and experience, your life's narrative and story lines are being built.

This storyline shapes how you interpret future encounters. Achieving aspirations, hopes, and dreams involves paying attention to your internal storyline and how you observe and interpret what has unfolded within and without you. Often our narratives ground our dreams and shoot down our aspirations. It is at these moments where we need a lifter to help us see beyond now and grow us to a point where we can reshape our inner dialogue and live above what we have or are going through. It is at this place where eternity invades my plans and goals.

Reframing allows you to experience a fresh new season by simply altering your thoughts. Sometimes, what you are looking to support you from your history won't be there since disadvantages affect everyone. Often, the difference isn't the perceived advantages/disadvantages but rather the ability to find a compelling destiny from your past.

We must resist the need to interpret our past as a failure.

What are the reasons you should fight to redefine a bad experience? To start with, failures like successes can leave an imprint on your perspective. Mis-interpreting an experience can alter your focus. Rethinking your mistakes and failures allows you to transform the experience into an incubator for learning, providing important feedback about what you were made for or what you were not made for. Each of those clues are needed going forward.

Another important point is, don't live out of a victimization paradigm. You cannot live on purpose and function out of an old paradigm. A paradigm is information placed within a framework which ultimately drives how you think and act.

- 🔎 Victimization paradigms always keep you focused on what you've lost.

- 🔎 Victimization paradigms blame others for your current position in life.

🔎 Victimization paradigms suppress the activation of your gifts, skills, and abilities and increases your desire to quit.

🔎 Remaining a victim always focuses on what was done to you or taken from you, but it's always unprofitable for you.

**Here's the good news!
I can't always choose what happens in life,
but I do choose my attitude.**

To live on purpose, I do not have to change my past, I simply have to re-interpret it. I can decide not to have an experience and leave empty handed.

Choices and Chances

At the age of fifteen, I came to experience one of the most difficult moments in my life. My father left our home to visit a friend's house a few miles away. By night fall, my life would be forever changed by the hammering of a fist on our front door, the voice of a sheriff speaking to my mother, and the sound of her screaming, "Not Earnest." Within the matter of a few hours, my father had been murdered by his friend and just like that, what I thought my destiny would be, was completely turned upside down.

From that moment until now, I have found that no matter where you are or what cards you've been dealt, life and destiny come down to two words, choices, and chances.

Choice is our ability to make decisions with respect to the options that are available to us. This is not about the psychology of choice which we've already discussed, but rather being motivated to decide. Choice is about the truth that we get to activate a move and do what is healthy for us.

Progressive Action:

Make a choice to be intentional and purposeful with where you invest your time, gifts, and your resources.

🔎 What choice do you need to make to create the future that awaits you?

🔎 Why is this important?

Since the future is created in the present, when you arrive in the future you call it today, but today is about choices.

Every choice that you make today meets you in the future and says, "Welcome, we've been waiting for you."

Now that we've discussed Choices, let's move on to Chances. What is interesting about the time we live in is, people are playing musical chairs with their futures, adverse to taking chances, resolving to go through life and come out empty handed. It reminds me of the game Musical Chairs I loved when I was a child. Musical chairs is when you go around and around to the music someone else is playing and when the music stops, if you do not take a chance then you don't have a seat. I encourage you to find the song/dream that makes your heart sing and soul come alive.

Progressive Action:

Take a **Chance** on your dreams because there will never be the perfect time to become the person you might have been.

🔎 Are you ready to take a chance on you?

🔎 Are you ready to take a chance and play your own music instead of risking being left without a seat when the music stops?

🔎 Are you committed to ensure you don't come out of this moment empty handed?

🔑 *Pause and Reflect…*

Review the Key Points highlighted in this chapter. Journal what revelation you received from each one and how it will affect how you look at and deal with change and disruptions in your life.

➤ **You cannot always control whether difficult things happen to you in life, but you can control, to a large extent, how you react to them.**

➤ **Substituting the word "feedback" for the word "failure" allows us to focus on improvements and modifications instead of loss.**

➤ **The question in life and business is not what happened, but what happened next.**

➤ **Pain-based decisions are the opposite of values-based decisions.**

➤ We must resist the need to interpret our past as a failure.

➤ Here's the good news! I can't always choose what happens in life, but I do choose my attitude.

➤ Every choice that you make today meets you in the future and says, "Welcome, we've been waiting for you."

Say Out Loud...

Learning happens with **Frequency, Intensity** and **Repetition**. So, this week, repeat these declarations loudly to yourself in front of a mirror at least 6 times daily.

❖ I will respond not react to crisis situations in my life.

❖ I do not have to change my past; I simply must interpret it.

❖ I can decide not to leave an experience empty handed.

❖ I will look through the lens of feedback not failure.

[Chapter 8]

RE-INVESTING PAIN AND DISAPPOINTMENT

Mercidieu Phillips

"A wise man will make more opportunities than He finds.
—Francis Bacon[31]

"In the middle of difficulty lies opportunity."
—Albert Einstein[32]

THE STORY READS like a fiction, but it is the vivid reality of a courageous young man's life. The details of Kemba's story demonstrate a deep truth that crisis moments can begin at birth. It is not just when something occurs in the course of one's life but can be the very foundation on which an entire life is built.

Kemba is a successful leader who has had the privilege of traveling the world speaking at major conferences and engaging with a variety of audiences. However, his life did not begin with a hint of any level of success. As the product of promiscuous father, he was born into a broken home from day one. The person he called mother was more of a guardian than an actual mother. After surviving the trauma of a per-mature birth, Kemba was entrusted to the care of a not so loving mom. She despised his presence as it reminded her so much of his absent father.

As she struggled to provide food and shelter for him, she often reminded him of the mistake that his birth was and the subsequent wishes that she should have left him to die in that neo-natal wing of the hospital. A week would not go by without him hearing how much of a burden he was to her. His mother not only verbalized this to him but made sure her actions matched what she said. He was punished in all ways. From the choice of the food he had to eat, to the clothes he was forced to wear, Kemba faced one of the most difficult lives you could imagine.

His behavioral issues at school did not help his fate with others either. Kemba often got into fights as he battled deep anger issues. The issues facing him were layered. He was not wanted at home, despised, and mocked at school, and flat out marginalized just about everywhere else including church. He was made fun of because of the abject poverty he knew as a daily reality. For him, a crisis was not an occurrence, but a reality that he was born into. His world was shaped by crisis and his drive today is fueled by those extreme circumstances.

As we sat in his office and talked, I could not help but glance at the fixtures on his wall. The presence of several earned degrees and many other accolades adorning his nicely arranged workspace informed me that this man had triumphed over the many obstacles thrown his way. Throughout the conversation, I quickly began making mental notes of the some of the factors I thought contributed to his success as well as that of so many others like him.

Four Powerful Observations

For the purpose of arming you for possibly the same result or better, I will use the remaining lines of this chapter to delineate four powerful observations I have seen evident in almost every one of the people who have successfully re-invested pain and disappointment.

As you read through this section, highlight or underline the points that will help you re-invest the pain and disappointments you have experienced on your life's journey.

#1: Purging

Whether we admit it or not, we are all repositories in motion! We knowingly or unknowingly carry a collage of thoughts, projections, words, and events that have taken place at some point in life. Some of these are good and some are not so good. One of the major challenges of our lives is the propensity to under evaluate the role that these deposits play in shaping the person we are today. Our tendency to simply view these as "things" that were said or "situations" that happened drastically cheapens the value of what they have left behind. It is for this reason I am submitting to your conscience the idea of purging.

By purging, I am referring to the process of voluntarily choosing to decisively reposition the placement of certain future derailing events as part of the journey towards better. This is not an invitation to forget, but one to repurpose. This powerful exercise paves the way for the possibility of numerous life-changing decisions. When successful purging occurs, creative ducts are opened and once scaled eyes are freed to see beyond the pain and into the limitless landscape of ideas and dreams.

Naturally, our preference is to ignore the potential of setbacks. We can either see them as lingering hindrances or launching pads to a dimension seldom explored. They are viewed as obstacle or opportunity.

Life's happenings all interplay with mental roadmaps. They serve as clearly marked traffic signals attempting to guide us away from a fatal and unwanted collision with failure.

The story of Kemba I used as the backdrop for this chapter is peppered with references to how he would repeatedly choose to not place his circumstances in an unusable box. Rather, he removed the soul stinging elements through mental purging while safeguarding the vital components to construct the platform on which he stands today.

To purge oneself of crippling experiences, it requires the reorganization of one's mental shelf by placing the necessary factors at eye level.

- Purging is about being more concerned with the recognition of freedom, direction, and destination.

- It is the process of actively visualizing a diamond in the rough and making the necessary effort to capture it.

- Purging involves hard decisions that sometimes include losing close relationships with people who can't understand your call to better.

- To effectively purge is to accept a trade-off.

Purging is simply the commitment to transition into greatness.

#2: Choice of the Ideal

"You can either be bitter or better because of this, Jeff!" These are the words uttered during a challenging coaching session with a client who was struggling with the recent betrayal of his longtime business partner. This is the intersection where most futures crash and burn. This is the place where victims or victors emerge.

In addition to our damaged emotions, a multitude of factors help determine our next step away from pain and disappointment including the following: socio-cultural upbringing, emotional intelligence, spiritual foundations, family dynamics, and a plethora of other factors. These often-overlooked realities play a major role in shaping our preferences and priorities. A person's preferences and priorities are normally a reflection of their hard wiring which takes place at the point of each painful or disappointing moment they incur.

The choice to be better instead of bitter is often the most unpopular one because of the hard work it requires.

Bitterness requires very little effort! In fact, it is the most convenient choice due to the lack of resistance it often faces. Some of the greatest human impacting organizations have been founded by people who experience great trauma through pain and disappointment, but instead, they chose to use that experience for the betterment of others.

A week before I wrote this chapter, I came across a story about Maurice Clarett, the star running back for the Ohio State University's 2002 national championship team. After a brilliant college career, Maurice didn't excel in the National Football League (NFL) due to multiple run-ins with the law. His life came to a standstill when he was arrested for a crime and sentenced to seven years in prison.

> *Most experts predicted NFL stardom for Clarett after he led Ohio State to a BCS national championship as a true freshman in 2002. It didn't work out as planned. In 2003, he was suspended for receiving improper benefits, and eventually was dismissed from the Big Ten school. He challenged the NFL draft eligibility rules and lost, was drafted by the Broncos in the third round in 2005, but never appeared in a game.*
>
> *His life went off the rails from there, sinking into alcoholism and a life of crime. He served 3 $^1/_2$ years in prison for armed robbery before*

remaking his life with a drastic 180-degree turn. In 2016, he founded the Red Zone, which provides counseling for both children and adults in Youngstown, Ohio, and is looking to build a facility for college athletes dealing with substance abuse, mental health problems or other issues.[33]

He knew then that something had to change. Several years after his release, he started sharing his story during speaking engagements with high-profile college teams and other organizations. He used the money he received from those events to launch The Red Zone, a behavioral health and substance abuse agency in his hometown of Youngstown, Ohio, which services adults and children.[34]

Those who choose better over bitter usually find themselves leading scores of people away from a life of inner devastation, operating freely to a place where meaning and destiny become guiding friends.

"I'm living proof that no matter where you start off at and no matter what you're going through, there's a way to gradually get to where you want to go."–Maurice Clarett[35]

#3: Discovering Purpose

In his runway best-seller, The Purpose Driven Life, Christian author, Rick Warren managed to strike a nerve with more than just those who confess to be

born again followers of Christ. His message resonated with people of different faiths and socio-eco-
nomic backgrounds. Why? Because he talked about
something that everyone is in pursuit of discovering,
purpose. From personal life coaches to marketing pro-
fessionals, people are being challenged to discover
their "why."

If you study life's varying cycles, you will soon discover
that everything that happens somehow comes back
around at another time to demonstrate that it wasn't
an accident. Covered underneath the rubble of hurt,
disappointment, and a gutted soul, is the seldom discovered gift of meaning.

> Meaning is that little element that provides
> the impetus for someone to seek more than
> what is readily available to the naked.

> Meaning creates a deeper well of much
> needed to quench the thirst often caused by
> a feeling of insignificance.

> Meaning is the imaginary glass ceiling cre-
> ated by difficulties and challenges.

> Meaning is the stronghold of low expecta-
> tion and releases the much needed flow of
> power, reason, and destiny.

**The vicissitudes of life will test the very
core of one's foundation and it will take
the acceptance of a deep sense of meaning**

to broker between the reality of the actual moment and the promises of a better future.

I had the privilege of securing a coaching contract with Salena, a client who grew up in a rural town in Florida. Their town was not known for much more than the great vegetables and produce they harvested each year. Her parents introduced her to the hard work that put food on the table for the family. Salena expressed how she always knew that the activities that occupied her summers and weekends were being used to lay a foundation of hard work that would eventually produce success.

While she could not understand why poverty and lack were family friends during her upbringing, she did know that they were not a death sentence. Her grit, grind, and no excuse attitude help shape a resolve that would not allow the forces of self-defeat to win. Through toughness, brokenness, and self-will, she managed to break through the stigma that nothing good could ever emerge from this community.

Today, she owns and manages several different business ventures and provides employment opportunities for some of the families currently living in that town. The call to come back and make a difference was birthed in the womb of pain, frustration, and resentment.

The unveiling of stories like this demonstrates the depth of decision. Since it is reasonable and logical to accept the reality of an unfair hand given to play with, it is even more powerful to witness the choice that someone makes when refuting the easiness of giving up.

If life is not void of hardship and disruptive moments, resolve and the pursuit of better must become part of the process that leads to triumph over trials.

#4: The R.O.I

In the world of business, you will often find executives talking about ROI which stands for Return On Investment. Any prudent investor wants to know what their profit margin is when investing in a project or company. They do due diligence in order to take a calculated risk that has the highest chances of yielding a lucrative and satisfying return.

In the same way, those who make the choice of to re-invest pain and disappointment by deciding to use it for the common good, can expect to have an ROI that cannot be measured by the frivolity of tangible things. This return is not just seen in the lives impacted, but through the multiplication of the good that emanates from those who choose to do so.

The common and collective experiences each person has with hardship can act as the thread that knits together those who emerge from pain and disappointment to success and significance.

The willingness to make good use of one's pain can be a gift to another person who meandered in massive confusion while

knowing there could be a greater use for their experience.

●— *Pause and Reflect...*

Go back through this chapter and write down those highlighted or underlined the points.

Now, write down how you are going to use this information to help you re-invest the pain and disappointments you have experienced on your life's journey.

_____

_____

_____

_____

_____

_____

Difficult moments are part of the human experience, but not the sum total. Do the wise thing and become an active investor. Your stakeholders gladly await you.

Review the Key Points highlighted in this chapter. Journal what revelation you received from each one and how it will affect how you look at and deal with change and disruptions in your life.

➢ Life's happenings all interplay with mental roadmaps. They serve as clearly marked traffic signals attempting to guide us away from a fatal and unwanted collision with failure.

➢ Purging is simply the commitment to transition into greatness.

➢ The choice to be better instead of bitter is often the most unpopular one because of the hard work it requires.

➢ Those who choose better over bitter usually find themselves leading scores of people away from a life of inner devastation operating freely to a place where meaning and destiny become guiding friends.

➢ If life is not void of hardship and disruptive moments, resolve and the pursuit of better must become part of the process that leads to triumph over trials.

➢ The willingness to make good use of one's pain can be a gift to another person who meandered in massive confusion while knowing there could be a greater use for their experience.

Say Out Loud...

Learning happens with **Frequency**, **Intensity** and **Repetition**. So, this week, repeat these declarations loudly to yourself in front of a mirror at least 6 times daily.

❖ I choose to be better not bitter.

❖ I will make good use of the pain I have experienced in life.

❖ I will seek to find the opportunity in my difficulties.

[Chapter 9]

THE RELATIONAL ECONOMY

Kelvin McCree

"Relationships are the only thing that matter in business and in life.
—Jerry Weintraub[36]

"Working together precedes winning together...collaboration is multiplication."
—John C. Maxwell[37]

YEARS AGO, MY mentor shared a story that really made me aware of how vital relationships were to our health, success, ability to identify blind spots in our lives, and leverage our own latent potential.

The Bridge Story

The story began with "two men who were fishing in a stream, when they noticed that a nearby bridge was falling apart. Every time a vehicle would drive across it, another piece would fall, and the entire bridge would shake dangerously. Finally, after a large truck passed over, the bridge completely fell apart in the middle. The two fishermen knew that if a car came around the bend, the driver would never know that the middle of the bridge was gone; the whole thing could come crashing down, damaging the vehicle, and injuring the driver.

One of the men looked at his friend and said, "We've got to do something. What would be the right thing to do?"

His friend thought for a moment and replied, "Build a hospital?"

The story my mentor shared with me underscores what the challenges are in how we generally view our relationships. We tend to only care about them when tragedy strikes. Whether we're too pre-occupied fishing or encumbered with building our staircase to success, our lives in many aspects are isolated from the greatest wealth we have, relationships. We must be vigilant of moments to care for and be cared for. Each of us has an ability to embed ourselves behind a wall of rationalizing that we can succeed or be happy without healthy, life giving relationship.

In reality, none of us has the capability of truly reaching higher heights or achieving greater levels of success without a healthy relational economy.

We all understand that we live in a fast-paced society as well as the fact that many families are struggling to simply make ends meet or are spread thin in one-parent households. It is also readily apparent that it can be a challenge to reach out into a community to give back.

On the other hand, one of the great joys of living is that we get the privilege of being with other people. Imagine being on this planet without anyone to talk to, hang out with, or get feedback from. I know sometimes we all like a little quiet time, some more than others, but truthfully, we were not designed to be loners. The desire to associate with other human beings, to belong to a group, and be accepted by loving people is a universal desire. This reality transcends race, culture, language, or geographical boundaries.

Pause and Ponder...

+ *Why are we so averse to developing and maintaining relationships?*

+ *Can I truly be at my best without allowing myself to be genuinely connected to others?*

+ *Can we as a team or society be at our best if we don't truly care for one another?*

This is why understanding what the Relational Economy is and why you should be invested in it is so important.

A Relational Economy Is...

A Relational Economy is defined as simply understanding and recognizing that our economic life is not simply **quantitative** but also **qualitive**. Understanding our lives are also **qualitive** allows us to see our lives within "networks," "connections," and "healthy relationships." This broadened understanding helps us to begin to see the role people play in our personal space and the interactions and relationships between us.

On the contrary, when we reduce our lives to **quantitative** meaning based on the size of our bank statements and the stocks in our portfolio, we tend to be more selfish and focused on the competitive aspects of humanity.

> **Robert Waldinger in his Harvard research on living healthy states, "Loneliness kills, it's as powerful as smoking or alcoholism."**[38]

Rethinking Where We Invest

One thing I've done for years is invest in the stock market. Let's consider you invested in a stock that was doing well, but wasn't providing you the return you desired. One day, you are made aware of a stock that could provide an equally or perhaps even better return on your investment. What would you do? Most likely, you would diversify your investment or at minimum, rethink where you were invested.

> **Healthy Relationships have a way of increasing our relational portfolio and even making us healthier and happier.**

Earlier, I referenced Robert Waldinger's Harvard study. Robert serves as a psychiatrist at Massachusetts General Hospital and is a professor of psychiatry at Harvard Medical School. As the lead professor, he gave oversight to a study in the Health and Medicine section of the Harvard Gazette entitled, "Good Genes Are Nice, But Joy Is Better." Research that began with 238 subjects in 1938 and lasted over "80 years as part of the Harvard Study of Adult Development" found, "embracing community helps us live longer and happier." Essentially, the research revealed that there is a direct correlation between the health of our relational economy and the health of our lives.[39]

The recent disruption caused by Covid19 has put all of humanity in a collective and congested cohort as a community of learners enrolled in an intensive fast track program. The two primary instructors of this program introduced themselves as Professors Quarantine and Shelter In Place. The medical experts leaned heavily on the premise that if people could manage to curtail their interactions, they would have a better chance at flattening the curve.

Looking beyond the scientific and personal benefits of adhering to those recommendations, one must see the relational benefits such a forced change provided. With school doors closed and companies putting scores of employees in furlough mode, families were forced to spend more time together. It was no longer the norm to operate like two ships passing in the night. More meals we consumed together as subscriptions to Netflix skyrocketed. Tech companies like Zoom and Facebook saw massive traffic on their platforms as people had to find creative ways to "connect."

The fundamental lesson to be learned was the indispensable truth that after all the

scientific and technological advances, we still need community.

The convenience of an expensive personal computer, smartphone, or tablet cannot substitute for the richness and depth of a human connection. The Covid19 disruption stripped us of all false pretenses that were carefully masked behind the Styrofoam walls of time, titles, positions, and social status. It heightened the need for a new relational economic stimulus check, a reality check!

The argument for willing, skillful, and generous investors in the new relational economy is simply an invitation into an extremely profitable venture that will yield both intangible as well as tangible dividends.

You Are Good for Me!

Another important layer of leveraging our relational economy is understanding the power and purpose of authentic and accountable connections.

Ask Yourself...

+ *Do I have authentic relationships with people or am I a filibusterer who talks well?*

+ *Am I really authentic with those I meet or call my friends?*

Research has shown the **quality** of our relationships can either enhance or hinder the quality of our health.

This raises an interesting question: Do authentic relationships contribute to better health? Strangely enough, a recent study reported almost 35 percent of those in excellent health had more than five close friends, which was the case for only 21 percent of persons who stated their health was either fair or poor. When we are engaged in authentic and accountable relationships, those interactions help to develop us and ultimately help move us into the person we are capable of being.

We all have heard of the phrase, "If it ain't broke don't fix it" and most understand it to mean if something is working well, don't change it. How can we apply this to being accountable to people? Each of us at some point will fall or be in relationship with someone who will. Anyone without a genuine relationship at the time of the fall will suffer more severely than they should and stay down longer than necessary.

Many people run from the idea of being a better person through accountability because of what they've seen in the past. It is vital we are cognizant of the fact our embracing of accountability is impacted by our views of it. If you or I have been disappointed in a relationship we've invested in, we are likely to see future relationships through that lens. As a result, we begin to gauge relationships by, "What's in it for me?" This ultimately moves us from a life of "we" to a life of "me."

Pause and Ponder…

✦ *Why do we have such difficulties in taking such an ideal Relational Equity of embracing the mutuality of our Relational Economy?*

✦ *What personal, cultural, or systemic blockages disable us from thinking in this new way?*

✦ *Why do practical examples like those shared earlier still leave us unconvinced that showing collaboration and co-operation are effective, even when there is strong evidence of positive benefits?*

✦ *Why does Relational Economy receive so little attention, remain unheard, on the margins, or is seen as exceptional?*

✦ *Why isn't it taught in our homes and discussed at our dinner tables?*

I firmly believe most of us want to grow, but I also believe that a core reason we pause at embracing this idea of investing in authentic and accountable relationships is due to not understanding how to structure relationships. Even more so, our society is not accustomed to being open to accountability and we are not trained on who to open our lives up to.

Below I have provided some structure on how to successfully recognize Relational Value and how to properly frame relationships with measured expectations.

Five Boundaries of Authentic and Accountable Relationships

1. Don't open your life up to people who are judgmental.

2. They will warp your view of others.

   - Judgmental people are often so because they are unable

- to find value and worth in others.

- Whether you are unforgiving toward yourself or connected to someone who is perpetually judgmental, there is always one through cord, you and your energy end up drained.

- Don't open your life up to people who are so deeply hurt, they are unable to move their minds or their mouths to help empower you or give life to a better you.

3. Don't open your life up to people who trample over what you find important.

   - Don't put what's important to you before people who don't value it.

   - If you de-value what I believe, I am involved with, or I like, it dis-allows you to love me.

   - People open up to people that respect their values.

4. Don't open your life up to people who turn flaws into personal attacks.

5. Don't open your life up to people who want to use you.

6. You want people who genuinely want you to succeed.

   - You want people who not only understand what a relational economy is, but understand the power of reciprocal engagement.

Close, authentic, accountable, and healthy relationships add value to us.

In this new economy, these life-giving relationships are more than money or fame and more valuable than any stock you own. Having a healthy Relational Economy aids in keeping people happy throughout their lives, protects us from life's discontents, and from slowing down our mental and physical capacity.

Since aging starts at birth, I encourage you to start taking care of yourself at every stage of life starting today. If you don't, you just may be leaving relational money on the table.

● *Pause and Reflect…*

Any wise investor will encourage you to do your research to better understand your investment. So, as you consider ways to tap into your own relational gold mine, here are a few questions you may want to consider.

✦ *Who are the people you trust?*

✦ *Who are the people you know who are already in authentic and accountability relationships?*

✦ *Who do you have a genuine relationship with and who fully grasps the concept of a relational economy?*

These questions are vital because those who understand "people wealth" are most likely to be honest with you and give you the greatest return on your investment into the relationship.

Review the Key Points highlighted in this chapter. Journal what revelation you received from each one and how it will affect how you look at and deal with change and disruptions in your life.

> **In reality, none of us has the capability of truly reaching higher heights or achieving greater levels of success without a healthy relational economy.**

> **Robert Waldinger in his Harvard research on living healthy states, "Loneliness kills, it's as powerful as smoking or alcoholism."[40]**

> **Healthy Relationships have a way of increasing our relational portfolio and even making us healthier and happier.**

> **The fundamental lesson to be learned was the indispensable truth that after all the scientific and technological advances, we still need community.**

> **The argument for willing, skillful, and generous investors in the new relational economy is simply an invitation into an extremely profitable venture that will yield both intangible as well as tangible dividends.**

> **Close, authentic, accountable, and healthy relationships add value to us.**

Say Out Loud…

Learning happens with **Frequency, Intensity** and **Repetition**. So, this week, repeat these declarations loudly to yourself in front of a mirror at least 6 times daily.

- ❖ I will invest in life-giving relationships.

- ❖ I will develop authentic and accountable relationships with those I can trust to value our relationship.

[Chapter 10]

ENJOYING THE FRUIT OF CHANGE

Kelvin McCree

"Adapt or perish now as ever, is nature's inexorable imperative."
—H.G. Wells[41]

"The secret of change is to focus all of your energy not on fighting the old, but on building the new."
—Socrates[42]

DUE TO COVID-19, graduations across the nation and world learned for the first time what a "Virtual Commencement Ceremony" was and looked like. We saw amazingly creative and ingenious ways high school seniors could be celebrated for this noble achievement. We witnessed a crash course in imagination from "drive-by ceremonies," to "honk-n-go" graduations, and still others done in the parking lots of outdoor movie theatres. We even saw one of my all-time favorites, graduations done in the aisle of major retailers like Target and grocers like Publix Supermarket. We also witnessed the first ever virtual commencement address given by the nation's 44th president, Barack Obama. Historically this moment for generations has marked the start of a promising future and crossing the threshold into adulthood.

However, not everyone embraced the moment. While many students enjoyed these unique celebratory displays that were forced upon them due to social distancing requirements related to COVID-19, not every high school senior could enjoy the fruit of change.

Opinion writer for the New York Times, Mary Retta quoted one student describing the moment feeling, "both a creepy post-apocalyptic exercise and a corny semi-pointless ritual" (NY Times Opinion "I Graduated Alone In My Pajamas").[43]

In May of 2020, I had the distinct pleasure of being invited to participate in the commencement ceremony for an educational institute's business cohort. As I was trying to find a message that would connect with the students at this pivotal juncture in their academic careers, I realized this moment encapsulates a key aspect they'll have to face for the rest of their lives.

In today's competitive market, we must not simply adapt to change, but learn to seek out the fruit of change.

For many of us, change is something we fear because it's disruptive. It forces us to shift our perceptions or approaches about what we do and how we go about doing it. At the very least, it leaves us questioning our current assumptions and how close they really are to reality. By allowing our minds to pivot toward discovering the benefits and fruits of change, we can celebrate this moment and the moments to come as important. If somehow, we could move from resisting change to understanding the very purpose of it and ultimately celebrating it, we are more likely to see our unexplored potential and under-appreciated fruit.

Consider how only fifteen years ago, no one knew what a tweet was. In 2004, Facebook only had 1 million users. Today, Facebook has 2.60 billion users and maintains 1.73 active daily users. You may remember when Facebook launched, the only thing we liked or understood to do was poke one another. Today, we can buy and sell, make calls, run ads, conduct meetings, and the list goes on. What originally was mainly a business tool and not a platform, we are now texting from our mobile phones.

Yes, a lot has changed in the world over the last year. As a result of COVID-19, much has changed in all our personal lives. Yet, despite the changes with Twitter, Facebook, Mobile Phones, and the changes related to COVID-19, we are all beneficiaries of the fruits of those changes.

Dreaming of fruit means you are thinking more about the benefits of a temporary disruption rather than the idea of being disrupted.

Looking Through the Rearview Mirror

➤ *What do you see?*

➤ *What have you learned?*

➤ *Where can this lead you?*

> *How have you grown?*

As we look through the rearview mirror of our lives, there is usually a common thread we all come to realize. Good things in life were often linked to change.

The Power of Visualization

The roles of thinking and feeling have become vitally important. When we think differently, it fuels behavioral change and leads to better results. As we take the time to understand and analyze change and think through it logically, we not only alter how we approach change, but subsequently change our behavior toward it.

Feeling differently about change can affect behavior and lead to better results. We can do this by using what is known as "The Power of Visualization." This technique has been used by Michael Jordan to increase the quality of his game and by Tiger Woods to increase the quality of his golf swing.

In 1996, at the University of Chicago, Dr. Blaslotto conducted a study by asking a group of randomly selected participants to take a series of free-throws. The percentage of free throws made by the students were tallied. The students were then divided into three groups and asked to perform three separate tasks over a thirty-day period.

The first group of students were prohibited from touching a basketball for 30 days, which essentially meant, there would be no practicing or playing basketball whatsoever.

The second group was permitted to practice shooting free throws for a half an hour a day for 30 days.

The third group were asked to come to the gym every day for 30 days and spend a half hour with their eyes closed, simply "visualizing hitting every free-throw."

After the 30 days, all three groups were asked to come back and take the same number of free-throws they had in the beginning of the study.

The first group of students who were prohibited from practicing or playing basketball at all showed no improvement.

The second group who were permitted to practice every day ultimately showed a 24 percent improvement.

However, the third who we're prohibited from touching a basketball or practicing but were simply focused on visualizing themselves successfully making free-throws, showed a 23 percent improvement.

Note well that the group focused on purely visualizing success had virtually the same measurable improvement as those who had physically practiced.[44]

The Power of Visualization is about creating surprising, compelling, and powerful visual experiences that allow us to taste the benefits of the fruit of change. As we begin internalizing in our hearts the fruit emerging from our stories and visualizations, we begin to feel differently about change and significantly improve our appreciation of it.

What are the fruits and benefits of change?

I believe there are seven fruits and benefits that change with disruption provide us if we only have the courage to clean our proverbial lens and look more closely.

1. **Personal Maturity** – We learn, scale our thinking, and mature every time we experience change. We find discoveries about ourselves and fresh new insights about all aspects of life. We learn what we're made for and even what we're not made for. These incremental steps are part of becoming more mature in how we will handle the next moment of disruption.

2. **Pliable** – Like a lump of clay in the hands of a skillful visionary potter, changes make us easily adaptable to new situations, new environments, and new people. As a result, we are no longer freaking out when there is a sudden shift or something happens unexpectedly.

3. **Enriched** – I am always looking for ways to improve, grow, and polish up. It may be about my finances, beautifying my home, learning new ways to be a better coach, or improving my relationship with my wife. We know none of these things improve themselves, so we need to do things differently to make that happen. Without change, nothing is enriched or improved.

4. **Life Values**–From time to time, changes make you re-evaluate your life and look at certain aspects from a different angle or through a slightly different lens. In these moments, we find our values being reinforced as a guide across unfamiliar thresholds.

5. **Getting Off the Treadmill** – Change gives us the opportunity to stop being like Darla, my son's hamster who spends what seems to be hours on her treadmill. One day, my son took her out and placed her on our living room floor to see how she'd respond. After surveying the new environment, she began to scurry around as if to say, "This freedom feels great." Without change, you'd be like Darla, living a predictable and uninteresting life.

6. **Forward Momentum**–Often we give up because we cannot accomplish the difficult task of making a huge and immediate change. That is when incremental pivots become extremely valuable. One shift at a time and small changes will eventually lead us to the desired big one. Changes trigger progress. Things move forward and develop because of them.

7. **Opportunities for New Beginnings**–One never knows what each change may bring. When you turn from your usual path, there will be plenty of different opportunities waiting for you. Changes will bring new choices for happiness and fulfillment. Each change is a turning page. As you acknowledge that this moment is about closing one chapter and opening another

one, you can begin to taste the new fruit that awaits you.

Commencement

Finally, I want to revisit the term commencement we used at the beginning of this chapter in order that we solidify and glean some purpose from it as it relates to the fruits of change. The very name commencement is actually a French word meaning to "commence" or "begin." Change is **not** about today. It is **not** about permanently parking to celebrate what you have accomplished. It is about leaning into what you are about to begin.

Today marks the beginning of the next chapter in your life where you will take the knowledge, experiences, and insights you've learned from previous moments of change and disruption and allow those to develop and help guide you on the path to that life you were meant to live. It is about becoming and coming into the person you were always meant to be. That is the fruit of change.

Write a chapter in your journal about the knowledge and insights you learned from the previous moments of change.

How have they helped guide you to become the person you are meant to be?

My mentor and motivational speaker Les Brown says, "Victory happens twice, first in the mind and then without."[45]

← *Pause and Reflect…*

See yourself not where you are, but on the other side of this disruptive moment. Make a commitment today to start envisioning the fruit of change in your mind, doing so makes the process of change less about what's happening to you and more about the fruit that will emerge on the other side.

Review the Key Points highlighted in this chapter. Journal what revelation you received from each one and how it will affect how you look at and deal with change and disruptions in your life.

> ➤ **In today's competitive market, we must not simply adapt to change, but learn to seek out the fruit of change.**

> ➤ **As we look through the rearview mirror of our lives, there is usually a common thread we all come to realize. Good things in life were often linked to change.**

> ➤ **My mentor and motivational speaker Les Brown says, "Victory happens twice, first in the mind and then without."[46]**

Say Out Loud…

Learning happens with **Frequency**, **Intensity** and **Repetition**. So, this week, repeat these declarations loudly to yourself in front of a mirror at least 6 times daily.

❖ I commit today to start envisioning the fruit of change in my mind.

❖ I will continue to take the knowledge, experiences, and insights I've learned to guide me on the path to that life I am meant to live.

[Chapter 11]

I GOT NEXT

Mercidieu Phillips

*"The entrepreneur always searches for change,
responds to it, and exploits it as an opportunity."*
—Peter Drucker[47]

*"If someone offers you an amazing opportunity
but you are not sure you can do it, say yes—then learn
how to do it later."*
—Richard Branson[48]

ON THE PLAYGROUNDS where I grew up, recreational centers were non-existent and that still remains the case today. My love and passion for the game of basketball were forged on the subpar outdoor courts. We played in any weather conditions, because we simply loved to "hoop" as boys. Each day, the number of young men waiting to play was more than the two lousy hoop fixtures provided. Teams were often picked by the first two players to arrive and everyone else had to sit and wait their turn. The password for having a chance to play at all that day was, "I got next!" These three words reserved a spot for the next team captain to pick his team while they waited to face the winner. During the waiting time, whoever had next would sit and watch the current game as a fan and a scout. This was done for two reasons.

First, you had to watch to see who was going to be on the losing end and whether or not any of those players could join your newly formed team.

Second, you watched to study the game plan, style of play, and schemes of the winning team. This data would assist you in picking the right players suited to attack and defend the winners. Winning meant everything, because the more resistant and successful team never left the court, even it meant playing all night. There on those courts, I learned a very valuable leadership lesson.

Success is not automatic! It has to be called out.

The Thrill of Going Next

In this chapter, I intend to highlight five dominant characteristics of those who will enjoy the privilege and thrill of "going next." Recognizing, accepting, and applying these known but seldom practiced habits will position you to experience a new normal that is synonymous with significance.

1.Willingness

An intricate part of the human soul is the will. The field of semantics for the term "will" shows several different ways one can define and interpret the concept. Some of words that are used to explain the will are, desire, wish, disposition, volition, inclination, etc. All of these terms are used to describe the fundamental function of the will. It is described as, "mental powers manifested as wishing, choosing, desiring and intending."[49] This is precisely what I believe the will is meant to do.

We have all no doubt heard the famous saying, "where there's a will, there is a way." This powerful phrase is a rendition of what was first introduced and published in 1640 in the work of Jacula Prudentusm produced by George Herbert. The original phrase read like this, "To him that will, ways are not wanting." The phrase re-worded or altered in the 1820's to read the way we know it.[50] A succinct understanding of the powerful phrase simply means that the true sponsor of any success is the will power of the person in that particular situation.

I want to revisit another basketball related story. On June 11, 1997, hall of fame basketball player, Michael Jordan played in what is now known as the "Flu Game." It was game five of the NBA Finals between his Chicago Bulls and the Utah Jazz. Both teams were tied at 2-2. This game was seen as the swing game in a best of seven series. The winner of game five has gone on to win 82 percent of the time.

Dealing with flu-like systems all day leading up to the game, everyone was concerned whether or not Jordan would play. Despite his depleted physical condition, Jordan suited up and joined his teammates on the court. At the onset of the game, it was quite noticeable that Jordan was not himself. He struggled to get up and down the court. His limited abilities afforded the Utah Jazz to get out front with a sixteen-point lead. As the television cameras focused on Jordan, he was seen with ice packs on his head and slumping back in his seat during timeouts. As players took free throws, he was often seen with his hands on his knees gasping for every bit of air he could. His consumption of fluids was extremely irregular that particular day.

At the start of the second quarter, the entire basketball watching world began to see flashes of the old Jordan. He torched the Jazz for seventeen points in that single quarter. The tension and level of nervousness was palpable in the Jazz's arena among the fans. Jordan didn't stop there. By the time the game ended, his box score read like something from a movie designed to showcase the star. Jordan scored thirty-eight points, seven rebounds, five assists, three steals, and one block. To make matters worse for the opposing team, he scored the go-ahead basket, a three-pointer with less than a minute left in the game. The Bulls escaped with a 90-88 win and went on to win their fifth championship.

After that "Flu Game," during an on-court interview, Jordan said, "I almost played myself into passing out. I came in and I was almost dehydrated, and it was all to win a basketball game."[51]

- The valuable lesson learned here is about the **power of the will**.

- **The will** is that inner push that **will not allow extenuating circumstances** to **rob you** of what is **potentially attainable**.

- **The will** is that rebellious voice that **refuses to accept no as an answer**.

- **The will** is that steady companion that **will not let you do anything less than pursue the win** that is within reach.

Ask Yourself: Will I be one of those who listens to my will and follow its leading?

Declare: I will join those telling the story of overcoming as opposed to being overcome!

The disruption of COVID-19 is a powerful extenuating circumstance with lethal effects. It is a silent enemy and a formidable foe. However, despite its devastating passage globally, it is a unique opportunity for those who will accept it as such.

The willingness to go beyond the seen into the unseen could serve as a catalytic force to launch one into a future ripe with the delectable fruit of prosperity and productivity.

2. Inspiration

As human beings, not human doings, we were created with the innate ability to live an inspired life. The spiritual aspects of our existence house the ability to live a life full of inspiration. All people, irrespective of their faith, find inspiration in stories with good endings.

There is something about the human soul that is pricked when we hear the accounts of how someone overcame an adverse situation. We cheer for the underdog who defeats a once overwhelming opponent. There are more fans who relate to David than Goliath.

- Challenges, disruptions, setbacks, and difficult moments are necessary to help you understand **the power of the potential you carry**.

- Inspiration is a manifestation of **accepted purpose**.

- Living an inspired life is like igniting a pile of coal that was created and designed to burn. The fire sparked by inspiration spreads like wild and holistically consumes those in its path.

The life lived through inspiration reaches for the promises of tomorrow by setting audacious goals.

It was Michelangelo who said, "The greater danger for most of us lies not in setting our aim too high and falling short; but in setting our aim too low and achieving our mark."[52]

Ask Yourself: Do I want to be among those who reach for the promises of tomorrow?

Declare: I will set audacious, high goals for my tomorrow!

The deficit of inspiration is very common and robs the individual of a life stuffed with endless dividends never presented for redemption. The bliss of the inspired life is loaded with endless offerings. To feel inspired is to feel life itself. To not feel inspired is almost equivalent to death. When we see the radiance of a face illuminated by our inspired life, it removes the hazard we once viewed as a life of trouble. The powerful spark of hope and the possibility of tomorrow creates an unbreakable agreement with the powerful feeling of unweaning desirous living.

The resistance to this life is often masked with the wrappings of incomprehensible pain, frustration, and scaled crises. The desire to go beyond the present must be fueled by an element of inspiration that flows from a life buoyed by the sheer determination to see an alternative. The inspired overcomer must first act within the parameters of how they were created to live.

God's first gift to man was the priceless ability of making him alive spiritually. The debate about faith or belief may be flooded by the plurality of choices available to the wanderer, but little argument can be made that man seeks to connect with something intangible that produces hope, meaning, and utter purpose.

Meaningful comebacks require the power of the will, the effort of the psyche, and the inspiration of the spirit.

Ask Yourself: Will I live the inspired life I've been created to live in lieu of the feelings of defeat clamoring for my being?

Declare: I will accept my personal invitation to this rare but precious sphere of being!

3. Discipline

Disruptions test discipline.
Discipline reveals priorities.
Priorities point to destiny.

Of all the scoreless responsibilities we have as human beings, none is more important or critical to our survival like discipline. The sudden presence of a crisis or moments of uncertainty induce a deep craving for the known comfort of nothingness.

- The discipline I argue for here is the **ability to resist the urge to settle** for the happenings of the here and now.

- Discipline is that **unique aptitude** that **refutes all** superficial and easy shortcuts.

- The wait to go next requires the **mental discipline** of following the actual game in play to observe and strategize on the adjustments that needs to be made.

Life is an ongoing exercise of adjustments. It is the stage on which we must practice the delicate dance of stability and agility.

Ask Yourself: Do I have the mental discipline to remain committed and focused on the bigger picture lying beyond the momentary disruption?

Declare: I will exercise mental discipline so I can experience the exuberance of staying with it!

The dichotomy of every challenge is never seen or known unless one enters into that space of situational navigation. By situational navigation I am referring to the interweaving of what is and what is to come. It is the art of correctly surveying the scope of an unwanted moment to properly obtain the necessary forward moving data while simultaneously deleting the potential elements of malware. Embracing the reality of the moment without being embraced by the moment is both a science and an art. It is the rare and exclusive lining that runs through successful person.

- Discipline is the **natural re-router** of the natural bent to choose the path of least resistance that we all possess.

- Discipline is the unseen thing that **keeps you on track** despite the non-cooperation of others.

An easy way to describe it is in thinking of a bumper rail as a bowling alley. When I first began my love and appreciation for bowling, I didn't know that you could choose to have the railing up to "bump up" your chances of hitting the pins. After discovering this disaster friendly option, I used it again and again until I became comfortable with my skills.

- Discipline is that thing **you must put up** as you navigate the bowling alley of life.

- Discipline helps with **ensuring** that you hit the pins and not veer of course.

- Disciplinc is the that factor that **lends a helping hand** in your pursuit of next.

Alone, it doesn't hand you "the next," but combined with a mindset and desire for better, it creates the pathway to attain your goals.

Though the choice is not hard, it will demand an exchange for its accompaniment.

4. Significance

Each year, I have the honor of working through a full schedule that takes me to many national and international destinations. During the keynote addresses or seminars I lend my expertise to, I will often refer to the four critical stages of achievement.

Note: As you read these four critical stages, discern which stage you are currently in and circle that stage.

First, there is the survival stage. This is where someone is just trying to make it to the next day. They are doing everything they can to keep themselves afloat. This is usually seen as the "by any means necessary" phase of life.

The second phase is success. Let me preface my thoughts here by acknowledging that success is indeed relative and not everyone defines it the same way. My personal definition and understanding of success are when you achieve a goal set by your own volition. You are successful when you maximize the opportunities presented before you. The inherent gifts and abilities are different for every person, therefore, it is only right to see success through the lens of what one is given to work with. For example, I can never consider myself less successful than Mark Zuckerberg or Tiger Woods.

What they have achieved in their respective careers is proportional to the platform they have been given. If I maximize my space by dominating the opportunities afforded, then I have achieved success.

Third comes the thriving phase. This is the evidence of having come through the survival phase and now they are displaying the visible evidence of that. The idea of thriving can be relative based on someone's interpretation of just what that means. When I speak of this phase, I am usually referring to the idea of someone who has successfully reached their cruising altitude and has leveled off. There is a rhythm to their life. They have proof that the hard work put in behind the scenes is has now paid off. Thriving means you are working a plan to near perfection. It simply means that you are experiencing a great amount of satisfaction for the time and effort invested.

The fourth phase is significance. This is the place where you work the "why" question. If you ever listen to those who are rich and famous, they will usually explain how they have become attached to a cause. This is when they start doing some "soul searching" to find meaning beyond their vast wealth.

People like Oprah Winfrey who launched a Leadership Academy for girls in South Africa in 2007. This boarding school for girls in grades 8-12 in the Gauteng province of South Africa is the result of her interaction with South African President Nelson Mandela. Oprah's "why" for starting this school was to help young girls who come from really poor and disadvantaged families, but who have a richness about their minds and future. It is a place for promise and capacity to be channeled towards greatness. Having grown up poor herself, Oprah saw this as a way to leave her fingerprints on girls who have the same start as she did, but could also experience the same finish she has experienced as a successful talk show host, actress, producer, publisher, media executive, and philanthropist.

Those who go next, never go there alone. They always take others with them because they understand one thing, significance is only achieved when the circle of beneficiaries is enlarged beyond just one person.

Call out your turn as "next" and invite others to come with you.

Who are you inviting to go with you?

5. The X-Factor

Every successful person will tell you they don't know how they did it. They just had an idea, worked it, and what you see is the result. While that may be true in part, I have come to realize that most people who experience significant success all possess something that isn't tangible to the naked eye. They normally have an ability to move out of some common present reality and into something that shifts their world. These are the people who create things out of nothing because of their rare ability to see not only what is happening in real time, but also the opportunities that can emerge from the now. The Cambridge Dictionary defines it as, "a quality that you cannot describe that makes someone very special."[53]

Today, everyone on the planet who has access to a computer or electronic device and the worldwide web has probably come in touch with the result of two audacious men who saw an opportunity and took it. If you have ever used the search engine known as Google, I am speaking about you. In the culture of Silicon Valley, California, there is a success story that should inspire anyone who is willing to dare to dream of possibilities. It is one of the stories that serves as potent smelling salt, strong enough to awaken a boxer who has been knocked to the ground by the vicious blows of a formidable opponent.

In 1998, two regular students at Stanford University in pursuit of their doctoral degrees in computer science found a way to enhance how people surf the web. While in a dorm room, they worked together to create an industry altering company. After successfully raising one million dollars from people who believed in their idea, Larry Page and Sergey Brin formed Google. By 2004, Google had already been recognized as a global giant. Their name and brand were unavoidable and would make its way from small towns all the way into government meetings.

They started with only three employees and worked out of a garage. They worked tirelessly to figure out a way to a more user-friendly advertising approach. They managed to discover how text ads that are not overly invasive could boost someone's search experience. They successfully made the company a necessity while creating a very profitable enterprise.

Six years after founding the company, Google went public and their stock became one of the most sought-after investment opportunities. Today, Mr. Page and Mr. Brin are considered as two of the most creative and wealthiest people on earth. Nestled in this amazing story is the X-factor they possessed. The Dot.com industry was already working long before they came up with Google, but they saw an opportunity to make it better and the X-factor in them propelled them to act on what was possible. In 2019, Google boasted a global workforce of 118,899 employees![54] Companies like Google are created by regular everyday people who see an opportunity and they act upon it.

Remember that the X-factor is described as "a quality that you cannot describe that makes someone special."

You have that one thing that makes you unique, too. Its power is creating a serious wave of tension in your mind. It is yearning to be released and explored for all it carries. Your X-factor is pushing you to have dreams without borders and to imagine a reach that is limitless.

Describe your X-factor:

_____

_____

_____

Your possibilities are endless if you can activate that dormant X-factor and get to work

on maximizing a disruption for an inevitable eruption.

● *Pause and Reflect...*

Review the Key Points highlighted in this chapter. Journal what revelation you received from each one and how it will affect how you look at and deal with change and disruptions in your life.

➢ **Success is not automatic! It must be called out.**

➢ **The willingness to go beyond the seen into the unseen could serve as a catalytic force to launch one into a future ripe with the delectable fruit of prosperity and productivity.**

➢ **The life lived through inspiration reaches for the promises of tomorrow by setting audacious goals.**

➢ **Life is an ongoing exercise of adjustments. It is the stage on which we must practice the delicate dance of stability and agility.**

➢ **Meaningful comebacks require the power of the will, the effort of the psyche, and the inspiration of the spirit.**

➢ **Those who go next, never go there alone. They always take others with them because significance is only achieved when the circle of beneficiaries is enlarged beyond just one person.**

➢ Remember that the X-factor is described as "a quality that you cannot describe that makes someone special."

➢ Your possibilities are endless if you can activate that dormant X-factor and get to work on maximizing a disruption for an inevitable eruption.

Say Out Loud…

Learning happens with **Frequency**, **Intensity** and **Repetition**. So, this week, repeat these declarations loudly to yourself in front of a mirror at least 6 times daily.

❖ I will activate that dormant X-factor in my life.

❖ I will call "next" and invite others to come with me.

❖ I will work to combine discipline with a mindset and desire for better to create the pathway to attain my goals.

❖ I will search for change, respond to it, and exploit it as an opportunity to move to my "next."

[Chapter 12]

TIME WAITS FOR NO ONE

Mercidieu Phillips

"Most people miss great opportunities because of their misperception of time. Don't wait. The time will never be just right."
—*Stephen C. Hogan*[55]

"Today is not just another day. It's a new opportunity, another chance, a new beginning. Embrace it."
—*Anonymous*

IT WAS 10:30 a.m. and I had just finished two very engaging online coaching meetings with a few business executives on my docket for that day. My cell phone kept buzzing during the coaching calls with the same number showing up each time. Immediately after wrapping up those calls, I decided to return the phone calls. It was another client who wanted me to get them a requested proposal that I had sat on for three full days. I have to admit, I was behind in a major way. The client said something that stuck with me. He was facing a deadline to apply for a State grant in excess of $750,000.00 and needed my figures to show where some of the funds would be allocated for executive and staff development.

As we exchanged some valuable information, he said, "Get this to me within the next three hours if possible because, 'Time waits for no one.'"

As simple as it sounds, this statement stuck with me for several reasons.

⌛ Time is the greatest asset each person has.

⌛ It is the one thing that can never be replaced because once it is gone, it never returns.

⌛ Time is God's gift that must be unwrapped if one is ever going to realize the beauty and significance of it.

⌛ If time remains closed to the naked eye and is never used effectively, its mere reality creates the mental logjam we commonly refer to as frustration.

⌛ Time is the first real capital that one has to invest in in order to pursue success.

It is critically important that the placement of time is done with much reflection, wisdom, and intelligence.

During an online Mastermind Course by my coaching firm, my co-author of this book, Kelvin McCree shared a powerful teaching about ensuring a platinum experience for the customers of any business. I caught the powerful truth of three simple words he shared. The words were **moments**, **mood**, and **memories**. For the sake of helping you process this concept of how time waits for no one, I would like to wrap your mind around those three concepts as we navigate this idea of time.

Navigate Moments:

The story has been told of how the late Senator Ted Kennedy of Massachusetts encouraged President Obama to run in 2008. Struggling with much reluctance about his electability because of his name, race, and experience, then Senator Obama didn't really think he could crack the election code. This is what Senator Kennedy said to him, "There are moments when you pick the time, and then there are moments when the time picks you. This is not your choice, but you have been chosen by this time."

Regardless of your political affiliation, Democrat, Republican, or Independent, these words ring true. We all know what happened following that challenge. Barack Obama, riding the wave of a nation ready for something new, became the forty-fourth man to hold the highest office in the land and secured his place in history as the first black President of the United States of America.

The global crisis known as Covid19 has no doubt created major disruptions to every layer of our civilized world. It has forced everyone who is willing to listen, to learn and understand the fragility of life and how nothing is ever an unshakeable reality. However, beyond the disruption, it has also been a moment where many companies and organizations can attribute their meteoric rise and huge profits. For example, tech giants such as Facebook, Zoom Communications, GoToMeeting, and even small web development companies have experienced tremendous demands for their services. They were strategically positioned to maximize this moment. Iconic chain restaurants found new ways to serve people who still placed a demand for their services through creative curbside services. Most businesses found new ways to capitalize on an unforeseen crisis by meeting the moment head on.

Moments in your life are like elevators. They take you to the level you desire by responding to the button you press. Not everyone riding the same elevator is headed to the same level. Some are going up while others are headed down. This moment is your elevator.

Look back carefully at your life...

❖ *Are you able trace some key moments that have shaped who you are today?*

❖ *Does remembering those defining moments provoke certain emotional responses from you?*

❖ *How did those moments contribute irreplaceable value to the progress of your reality today?*

The level you choose is totally up to you. The motivator in me is silently and cautiously hoping you choose the higher-level option that is readily available to you.

This is your moment! How will you navigate through it to ride the crest of the wave?

Navigate Moods:

During a 365-day year, I normally travel at least for 250 of those days. This means I spend a lot of time at airports, on airplanes, and in hotel rooms. Something always captures my attention when I check into the hotel that will serve as my "man cave" for the number of days I am in that city. I always try to get a sense for the mood that the hotel management and staff are looking to create. Some hotels have a waterfall type effect as you pull up to the front door or in the lobby. Others have very soft non-intrusive music playing in the background, while some may even have a live band to greet you.

When I get into the room, especially at the higher end hotels, there is usually some music playing and a welcome message on the television with my name displayed. Some will place a written personalized message from the management and some expensive chocolate on the pillow. All these efforts are done to create a certain type of mood for the time I will be spending there.

A mood is defined as "a conscious state of mind or predominant emotion; a temporary state of mind or feeling."[56] Let's break this down a little further. Events, occurrences, disruptions, and shifts all contain certain elements that contribute to your mood.

Every major life altering occurrence embodies a certain mood that will land on you in whichever way to decide.

List three major life altering occurrence you have experienced:

_____

_____

_____

Now draw a simple emoji expressing your mood during each event.

Some people make the unwise choice of becoming angry, frustrated, and despondent during a crisis. They allow the weight of the moment to sit upon their life with the crushing effects of a sandbag.

☹ This creates an emotional posture of sagginess.

☹ This disposition prohibits the penetration of hope and aspiration.

☹ The danger of accepting this mood to guide them is that it usually leads to a place of depression and despair.

On the other hand, there are some who choose to seize the moment as a mood swinger. They prefer to take it as their opportunity to crossover from a bad mood to a good mood. They envision the crisis as a golden opportunity to do something that has been delayed for a while.

☺ Their mood is usually upbeat and positive as they search for the diamond in the rough.

☺ These are the people who will make the choice to launch a new business idea or find an investment opportunity to collaborate on.

Your mood during a certain time will be a major player on what happens both during the crisis and after the experience. It is critical to guard your mood and to re-direct it towards a progressive curve, rather than allow it to point backwards. The forward pointing mood serves much like a favorable wind caught by the sails of a boat on the water. It gives it that much needed push towards the finish line. A positive mood in a difficult situation in real-time, eradicates the contrary effects of the moment.

Time carries moods, moods carry change, and change will carry you! Make the wise choice of deciding the mood that leads and does not drown.

Navigate Your Memories:

The images of planes flying into buildings as the skyline turned grey with the mixture of jet fuel, smoke, ashes of crumbling buildings, and the fire consuming an entire section of one of America's busiest cities is forever engraved in the memory of everyone who saw it. As President George W. Bush stood on the rubble with a bull horn in his hand, he declared that the USA will seek retaliation and shall never forget what just happened. It was a time of great chaos, but also an eternal deposit into the collective memory of an entire nation.

Crises creates memories that are difficult to shake. There is something about the makeup of our brains that registers the details and power of major events. Psychologist and psychiatrists note that our capacity to remember events happens as early as two years of age.

"Neuroscientists have discovered that when someone recalls an old memory, a representation of the entire event is instantaneously reactivated in the brain that often includes the people, location, smells, music, and other trivia. Recalling old memories can have a cinematic quality. In a new study from University College London (UCL), neuroscientists discovered that when someone tries to remember a singular aspect of an event from his or her past—such as a recent birthday party—that a complete representation of the entire scene is reactivated in the brain like pieces of a jigsaw puzzle coming together to create a vivid recollection. The new research reveals that humans remember life events using individual threads, that are coupled together into a tapestry of associations. In a press release, lead author Dr. Aidan Horner from UCL Institute of Cognitive Neuroscience explains, 'When we recall a previous life event, we have the ability to re-immerse ourselves in the experience. We remember the room we were in, the music that was playing, the person we were talking to and what they were saying. When we first experience the event, all these distinct aspects are represented in different regions of the brain, yet we are still able to remember them all later on.'»[57]

Memories are constant companions that serve as reminders of where we have been and what has happened in us. They should never be discarded or cheapened because they are the pillars that uphold the trusses of our hope and destiny.

A negative memory ushered into a positive mind is continually re-oriented in the direction of better, greater, and significance.

A person who has repeatedly guarded their mind from the abyss of negative thoughts that are trying to feed an afflicted self-worth gains a great advantage in the game of life beyond the norm. The ideal liberation of life happens when we voluntarily release the sting and grip of a negative memory in order to lay hold of a more promising future.

On the other hand, a negative memory placed in a negative mind only compounds the complexity of a life longing to experience freedom. Events, crises, trauma, and pain are all markers that hold a significant place in our journey. While they secure their place without much warning or advanced notice, their placement and prominence can be determined by the person they seek to dominate. This is the pressing dilemma for all who experience disruptions and major shifts.

The reality of the moment lived cannot be denied and the power of the future it holds shouldn't be denied either. The ultimate choice is squarely in the hands of the individual who must masterfully broker the transaction between memories that provoke growth and those that prevent development.

Moments can bring lasting memories of fear, anxiety, and disappointment. Nevertheless, moments can also birth new hope, meaning, and boldness.

The freedom to choose how you will respond to the demands of this new space is the key you hold to unlock vaults of hidden treasures.

● *Pause and Reflect...*

Review the Key Points highlighted in this chapter. Journal what revelation you received from each one and how it will affect how you look at and deal with change and disruptions in your life.

> ➤ **It is critically important that the placement of time is done with much reflection, wisdom, and intelligence.**

> ➤ **Every major life altering occurrence embodies a particular mood that will land on you in whichever way to decide.**

> ➤ **Time carries moods, moods carry change, and change will carry you! Make the wise choice of deciding the mood that leads and does not drown.**

➢ A negative memory ushered into a positive mind is continually re-oriented in the direction of better, greater, and significance.

➢ Moments can bring lasting memories of fear, anxiety, and disappointment. Nevertheless, moments can also birth new hope, meaning, and boldness.

Say Out Loud…

Learning happens with **Frequency, Intensity** and **Repetition**. So, this week, repeat these declarations loudly to yourself in front of a mirror at least 6 times daily.

❖ I possess the freedom to choose how I will respond to the demands of this new space created by this crisis.

❖ I hold the key to unlock vaults of hidden treasures within this crisis.

❖ I choose to make the wise choice of deciding the mood that leads me forward.

FINAL CHARGE

AT THE ONSET of this journey, we made it clear that our hope was for this book to serve as a much-needed jolt to awaken in you those possibilities that unwillingly lie dormant. We have invested the thoughts and reflections produced by the countless hours of deep reflection and research into this book. We are readily cognizant that the pages you have just interacted with are not a full and comprehensive prescription that will cure all the maladies that a crisis creates. Further, we admit that the truths shared by themselves are not sufficient to undo the stinging pangs of a disruption of this magnitude.

However, we do put forth with confidence that if you would simply create a small opening in your mind that would make room for new possibilities birthed out of an impossible situation, we believe you can become part of the exclusive community of difference makers. We strongly believe that you are strategically positioned to go beyond any previously explored places. Our deep-seated conviction strengthens our resolve that this unprecedented moment will create bottomless energy, infuse a newness to your step, and procure an unmitigated audacity to crush barriers.

As we repeatedly visited the premise for this book, the thought of helping and partnering with you kept reappearing as the sole motive. Your unlimited potential and borderless reach kept flashing before us in the similar way lighting flashes across a dark and gloomy sky. We felt the fresh droplets of the rain of hope. The wind of change is blowing in your direction and we are selfishly hoping you will ride its currents into the next season that is waiting on you.

In this book, we sought not just to embrace the fullness of Covid19 and all the newness it has created, but to create a new pair of glasses through which you can view the endless movements of success, prosperity, and abundance. We have not totally minimized the behemoth size of the present moment nor have we successfully eradicated the jagged edges of the memories it has created. However, we tried extremely hard not to embody an attitude that sponsored the common temptation of viewing this disruption as a setback. Instead, we optimistically view this as a set-up for a great comeback.

We engaged in this work to put forth the truth that is shared in, "Becoming a Resonant Leader" written by Annie McKee, Richard Boyatzis, and Frances Johnson. Because their words best explain our deepest sentiments, we invite you to read them:

> *"As a leader, no matter what your job or role in life, you touch people. You have the capacity to create wonderful, vibrant environments that make important differences in the lives of whom you touch. You can bring hope while also bringing results.... The best leaders move people. They*

engage people's heart and minds and help direct people's energy, individually and collectively, towards a desired end. And resonant leaders create a climate ripe with enthusiasm, hope, mutual support, and commitment. In other words, they lead with emotional and social intelligence and create resonant climates that can and do support both leaders and followers as both groups engage in the hard work of achieving goals and bringing about change."[58]

In this book, we have invited you on a journey that takes you from the doorsteps of a global pandemic and a major disruption, to the apex of possibility by seeing yourself as a difference maker.

The notions set forth before you are some of the practical tools we thought you could use to plow your way to a much broader horizon ripe with success.

The suggested idea of mental agility is designed to be a sword in your hands as you slice through the thick density of resignation and complacency.

The combination of research and real-life stories were meant to stimulate your desire to explore what's next.

We prayerfully hope you have found a renewed source of energy to transform your current situation, not just into the one you've always wanted, but the one you deserve. There is the belief in us that your passion, drive, focus, and aspirations have been ignited to launch you to a place beyond what has been and into what can be.

You can be the person who navigates this moment and brings others along for the experience. You were created for such a time as this and we remain confident that our small offering through these pages has provided the reminder and trusted companion you need to go and change the moment into momentum.

Navigate beyond!

ABOUT THE AUTHORS

Dr. Mercidieu "Phil" Phillips is a servant leader who seeks to add value to others through teaching, coaching

and equipping. He is a much sought after conference speaker, accomplished entrepreneur and executive business coach/ consultant.

He is the Founder and CEO of Level Up Coaching Solutions, LLC. Also, he is the founder and president of Level Up Leadership Institute, Inc.

In additional to his affiliation with the John Maxwell Team, he holds various certifications in Leadership and organizational development. Since 1990, Dr. Phil has successfully trained more than 175,000 leaders and organizations worldwide. Dr. Phil simply enjoys adding value to others. He and his family enjoy calling Southwest Florida home.

Kelvin McCree is a mental agility practitioner, focused on helping companies and organizations cultivate an agile workforce.

He serves as the Chief Learning Officer of Laser Focus Leadership Solutions and is the founder of the 8 Organizational Brand Pillars System, a system that assists businesses with developing and strengthening structural and staff engagement pillars around a consistent brand message.

He has served on numerous organization boards and as an advisor for Republican and Democratic Mayors.

Kelvin is a native of St. Petersburg, FL, and currently resides in the Central Florida region with his beautiful wife Evette McCree. They have one adult daughter, a teenage son, and three grandchildren. Kelvin's upbeat personality is seen through his signature greeting, "It's a great day!"

ENDNOTES

1 https://www.brainyquote.com/authors/
abraham-maslow-quotes

2 en.wikipedia.org/wiki/Awareness

3 www.businessballs.com/leadership-models/
four-frame-model-bolman-and-deal/

4 www.habitsforwellbeing.com/20-wayne-dyer-quotes

5 www.kotterinc.com/book/leading-change

6 Anxiety Tied to Stroke Risk in Study, HealthDay
Reporter

7 https://www.webmd.com/heart-disease/guide/
stress-heart-disease-risk

8 Reference: medicinenet.com/stress_and_heart_disease/
article.htm#:~:text=If%20stress%20itself%20is%20a%2

9 https://www.webmd.com/heart-disease/guide/
stress-heart-disease-risk

10 www.azquotes.com/quote/397001

11 "Can you Drink this Cup," p. 30

12 https://us.myprotein.com/thezone/training/much-americans-spend-health-fitness-survey-results-revealed/

13 succeedfeed.com/chris-gardner-quotes

14 www.goodreads.com/author/quotes/3047. John_F_Kennedy

15 https://www.princeton.edu/news/2017/08/02/princeton-researchers-show-how-brain-breaks-down-events

16 www.goodreads.com/.../quotes/4491185. Steve_Maraboli

17 www.azquotes.com/author/16182-Zig_Ziglar

18 www.physicsclassroom.com/class/newtlaws/Lesson-1/Newton-s-First-Law#:~:text=Newton%27

19 www.brainyquote.com/authors/seth-godin-quotes

20 Adapted https://en.wikipedia.org/wiki/WilliamWilberforce

21 Adapted from https://en.wikipedia.org/wiki/Martin_Luther_King_Jr.

22 Adapted from https://en.wikipedia.org/wiki/Nelson_Mandela.

23 Adapted from https://en.wikipedia.org/wiki/Mother_Teresa

24 Adapted from https://en.wikipedia.org/wiki/George_W._Bush

25 Adapted from https://en.wikipedia.org/wiki/Steve_Jobs

26 https://www.goodreads.com/author/quotes/44567.
Theodore_Roosevelt

27 https://www.mrlocalhistory.org/howardjohnsons/

28 https://www.tribstar.com/news/local_news/take-care-
of-your-mental-health/article_f70eaefb-378c-567f-
b242-80fb9aff567f.html

29 www.brainyquote.com/authors/tom-peters-quotes

30 www.goodreads.com/author/quotes/756.
Warren_Buffett

31 www.goodreads.com/author/quotes/50964.
Francis_Bacon

32 www.goodreads.com/author/quotes/9810.
Albert_Einstein

33 https://nypost.com/2020/06/27/maurice-clarett-turn-
ing-life-around-as-consultant-for-uconn-basketball/

34 https://www.espn.com/college-football/story/_/
id/28490590/inside-latest-chapter-former-ohio-state-
star-maurice-clarett-life-turnaround

35 https://www.espn.com/college-football/story/_/
id/28490590/inside-latest-chapter-former-ohio-state-
star-maurice-clarett-life-turnaround

36 www.goodreads.com/.../quotes/3371124.
Jerry_Weintraub

37 www.goodreads.com/author/quotes/68.
John_C_Maxwell

38 https://news.harvard.edu/gazette/story/2017/04/over-nearly-80-years-harvard-study-has-been-showing-how-to-live-a-healthy-and-happy-life/

39 https://news.harvard.edu/gazette/story/2017/04/over-nearly-80-years-harvard-study-has-been-showing-how-to-live-a-healthy-and-happy-life/

40 https://news.harvard.edu/gazette/story/2017/04/over-nearly-80-years-harvard-study-has-been-showing-how-to-live-a-healthy-and-happy-life/

41 www.goodreads.com/author/quotes/880695.H_G_Wells

42 www.goodreads.com/author/quotes/275648.Socrates

43 www.nytimes.com/2020/05/28/opinion/coronavirus.

44 www.philcicio.com/power-of-visualization

45 www.goodreads.com/author/quotes/57803.Les_Brown

46 www.goodreads.com/author/quotes/57803.Les_Brown

47 www.goodreads.com/author/quotes/12008.Peter_F_Drucker

48 www.goodreads.com/.../quotes/115943.Richard_Branson

49 Merriam-Webster.com

50 grammarist.com/proverb/where-theres-a-will-theres-a-way/#:~:text=The%20sentiment%20of

51 Theundefeated.com

52 www.goodreads.com/author/quotes/182763.
    Michelangelo

53 dictionary.cambridge.org

54 https://www.thoughtco.com/who-invented-goo-
    gle-1991852#:~:text=The%20very%20popular%20
    search%20engine%20called%20Google%20
    was,that%20a%20se

55 www.pinterest.com/pin/369928556879993258

56 Merriam-Webster.com

57 https://www.psychologytoday.com/
    us/blog/the-athletes-way/201507/
    the-neuroscience-recalling-old-memories

58 Published February 5th 2008 by Harvard Business
    Review Press